CATAMARAN SAILING

Derek Kelsall

Helmsman Books

First published in 1992 by
Helmsman Books, an imprint of
The Crowood Press Ltd
Ramsbury, Marlborough
Wiltshire SN8 2HR

British Library Cataloguing in Publication Data

A catalogue record for this book is available from the British Library

ISBN 1 85223 708 2

Acknowledgements

Thanks to James Boyd for the photographs appearing on
pages 19, 26, 35 (bottom), 42, 44 (top left), 96 (top), 108 (bottom)
and 109 (bottom).
Line-drawings by Claire Upsdale-Jones.

Throughout this book the pronouns 'he', 'his' and 'him' are used to refer to both men and women.

General Note
The yacht is normally referred to by its length overall. In the formulae and in the comparisons, we use the length on the water-line.
    GRP is used as an abbreviation for both glass-reinforced plastic and glass-reinforced polyester. Either would be correct but I prefer to use glass-reinforced polyester as it is more specific.

Typeset by Avonset, Midsomer Norton, Avon
Printed in Great Britain by Redwood Press Ltd, Melksham, Wilts.

CONTENTS

A Kelly 45 – with great stability and deck space.

INTRODUCTION

Britain's harbours are enriched by a wide variety of yachts and small boats that have been produced during the last one hundred years, including everything from old gaffers to the sleekest racing yachts. It has, however, taken catamarans (or cats) a long time to reach their present level of popularity, but they have now earned their rightful place among this wonderful mix of styles.

The general sailing fraternity is conservative almost in the extreme. Changes happen relatively slowly, but perhaps with some justification considering the dangers that can be faced off-shore. The belief that a sailing yacht had to be self-righting, with a heavy keel to be seaworthy was perhaps the major reason for the slow acceptance of catamarans onto the modern sailing scene. However, it is now evident in virtually all the harbours in Europe that the catamaran is increasingly being chosen to fill the role of sailing cruiser. Thirty years ago a catamaran was thought of as a strange craft; twenty years ago the catamaran was considered a novelty; today, however, it is an accepted member of the sailing scene, and even the smallest harbour or mooring will have one or two examples. Similarly, twenty years ago only the specialist yachting magazines featured multi-hulls, but today catamarans appear in features in all yachting magazines, and the specialist magazines are much more widely read.

Sailing yachts are classified as either mono-hull, reliant on ballast for stability, or multi-hull, reliant on wide beam, straddle stability. Multi-hulls come as catamarans (with two equal hulls), trimarans (with a main hull with two smaller outriggers) and proas (with floats and a main hull, and one smaller outrigger on one side). Of the three types, the catamaran is by far the most numerous in Europe today, so this book will concentrate on the role of the twin-hull as a sailing cruiser. However, there will be some reference to the other two types, and particularly to the trimarans as they have played a part in the acceptance of the general concept of unballasted sailing yachts.

A student of the sailing scene in the western world today could easily imagine that the catamaran was an invention from the 1950s and 1960s. This is, however, very far from the truth. It is almost certain that most early boats were either catamarans or outrigger craft – for example, most of the Pacific Ocean is populated with such craft today, and these will have certainly been sailing those waters since early times. It is very easy to imagine an early ancestor stepping on to a floating log, rolling off and immediately lashing two logs together to make the first catamaran. I maintain that far from being an oddity, the catamaran is a more natural sailing craft than one weighed down with lead, iron or rocks.

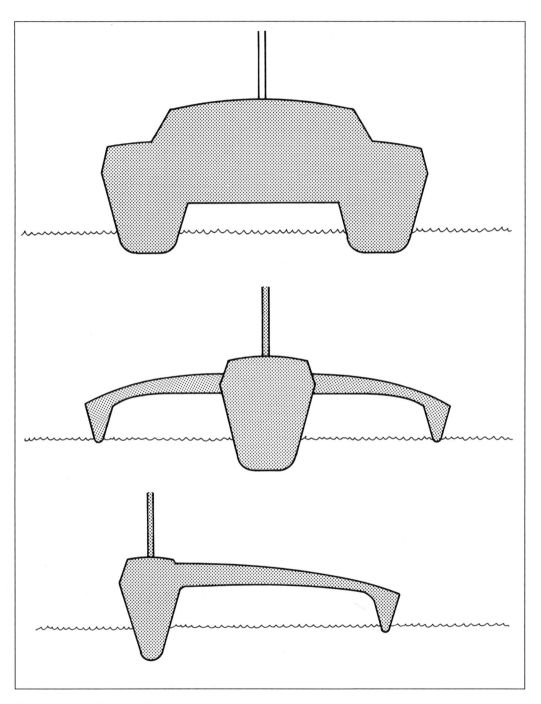

The catamaran, trimaran and proa.

Over the past 100 years, catamarans have been sailed occasionally in Europe, but it is hard to see just why it took until after World War II for any real development to occur. Over the past thirty years catamaran production has grown to perhaps 3–5 per cent of current yacht production in Europe. A similar situation exists in Australia, but catamarans in North America are still quite rare by comparison. Why should this be so?

As mentioned earlier, in the past there has been a certain amount of prejudice against cats amongst the established yachting fraternity. Multi-hulls aroused comments such as: 'does not go to windward', 'breaks up', and 'capsizes' – all commonly held views. The catamaran owner was seen as something of an oddity, prepared to risk the lives of all those aboard a yacht that was not self-righting. (Some of the early designers and multi-hull enthusiasts did little to help their cause, however, with greatly exaggerated claims for performance, ease of handling, low cost of building and so on . . . the boats did not always live up to these claims.)

From my own experience, when I was the first to sail a non-ballasted yacht (trimaran) in the 1964 OSTAR, it was reported in a major Sunday newspaper that my tri would 'straddle two waves and break up'. Today such criticisms and comments are rarely heard and the multi-hull (and the catamaran in particular) has earned its place on the water.

Catamarans are being built in considerable numbers today and there is no doubt that they are destined to become even more popular. If one needed confirmation of the trend towards twin-hulled craft, it is worth looking at other areas where the catamaran has also gained acceptance.

One such area is the passenger-carrying ferry industry where a high proportion of new ferries are catamarans, particularly the higher speed ferries. This development has been quite spectacular, all happening within the last ten years. Another area contributing to the general acceptance of catamarans is the situation in most holiday resorts. There are catamarans for hire on the beach, catamarans taking passengers on day-trips and catamarans on charter to parties who want to spend their vacations on the water. Couple this with the speed, excitement and popularity of the day cats, and there can be no doubt that future generations of sailors will find the catamaran concept most acceptable.

During the past three decades of the modern development of the catamaran, many ideas and features have been tried and tested. Today, designers are in general overall agreement on which features are most effective, and we genuinely can say that the cruising cat has come of age.

Whether your aim is to sail to far horizons or to own a yacht as an alternative to a country cottage, two hulls could suit you better than one and should be considered. This book sets out to explain the basic concept of the catamaran in simple terms, to illustrate what the catamaran has to offer as a sailing cruiser, and to outline what to look for in choosing a catamaran and what to expect when sailing one.

My own interest in sailing was first roused when I read *Treasure Island* and *The Kon-Tiki Expedition* as a youngster, but it was many years later that I was able to make my first off-shore passage to cement that interest. The departure point was Galveston in the Gulf of Mexico, the destination was Majorca and the yacht was a rather heavy 10m (32ft) trimaran. I had

A Kelly 45 joins an Iroquise Picnic gathering on the Solent.

sailed lots of small dinghies and cats on lakes and harbours, and the tri just seemed a natural choice for me. I have since designed, built, cruised and raced all types and believe that each has its place. I now specialize in designing cats, and I can see a very bright future ahead as more catamarans go afloat.

1
HISTORY OF THE CATAMARAN

The catamaran configuration goes back to early man, who (as mentioned in the Introduction) probably tied two logs together for stability, and thus created the first catamaran. Because the logs were too heavy to pull up the beach, early man then hollowed them out to leave a lightweight shell. The shell could then be paddled with ease at good speed and the dug-out hulls could carry a good load. An efficient vehicle had arrived on the scene. The obvious alternative to the catamaran with two equal hulls was the single dugout with a smaller outrigger which was used to give stability but not to carry loads. Others used double outriggers which were found to be most effective when using sails. Some of these early craft were built up to 30m (100ft) in length.

Examples of catamarans, single outriggers and double-outrigger craft can be seen today on the beaches of most Pacific islands as the working craft of the area. For instance, in some parts of the Philippines you can find, quite literally, hundreds of double-outrigger fishing boats operating off a single beach. They are used with great efficiency, being paddled, sailed or fitted with motors, and are used for carrying people, for fishing or just for pleasure. All the elements of an efficient catamaran can be seen in these outriggers

which originated over 1,000 years ago – two slim hulls, light weight and so on – from which the modern western catamaran differs only in detail.

In contrast to the Pacific islanders, however, the developers of the western world appear to have ignored the catamaran's potential. Isolated examples were built during the two or three centuries up to World War II, but none of these lead to any follow-up or real interest until after the war. A few of the notable examples, however, are as follows:

1662 – Sir William Petty produced a 6m (20ft) catamaran with cylindrical hulls which won a number of races. Other designs followed but some were very heavy and difficult to control.
1876 – the 7.6m (25ft) Nathanial Herreshoff design was built in the US. Other designs followed and managed to beat much larger yachts but were banned from racing by the New York Yacht Club as having an unfair advantage.
1936 – a 12m (39ft) catamaran was built in Hawaii and sailed to France by Eric de Bischop.

With the benefit of hindsight and with the exception of the Herreshoff design, perhaps the main reason why these cats did not show promise and encourage further development was that they tended to lack the important ingredient of light weight.

By comparison to the early years, the modern development could be described as rapid, but it certainly has not been as rapid as some of those directly involved would have liked to have seen or even expected. That such a simple and basic idea, with thousands of examples already existing in the Pacific Ocean, should have awaited western development until the era of the jet airliner, supersonic Concorde, the landing of a man on the moon, the computer and the robot is difficult to explain.

Perhaps one reason for its rapid development is that the last forty years have seen major changes to the overall sailing scene, particularly in the numbers of those participating. Also, even though yachts are still far from cheap, the use of mass-production methods and new materials has brought the cost of ownership within the reach of a greater proportion of the population than at any previous time. The facilities for yachts of all kinds are continuously expanding.

Any new type of craft has to prove itself first before any market for it will develop. During the late 1950s and early 1960s there were a number of pioneers who can rightly claim to have been instrumental in promoting the concept of unballasted sailing craft as seaworthy yachts. A few names – Roland and Francis Prout and James Wharram in the UK, and Jim Brown and Arthur Piver in the US – were responsible for getting a number of craft built and proved their ability to cross oceans in safety. James Wharram built his first catamaran and sailed it to the West Indies in 1958, while the Californian, Arthur Piver, built a number of trimarans which he campaigned in both the Atlantic and the Pacific oceans in the late 1950s and early 1960s.

A few major races then became open to multi-hulls and other names came to the fore – for example, Dick Newick, Rudy Choy, Derek Kelsall, Lock Crowther and Rod McAlpine-Downie. Starting in the early 1960s, the rules for some prominent races allowed any type of craft to enter and the main prizes were allocated on a first to finish basis. This was just what the cat and tri enthusiasts needed to put their ideas to the test. There were a few set-backs initially, but over a period of a dozen years these races proved the overwhelming superiority in performance of cats and tris, and silenced the critics who claimed that the cat and tri could not cope with conditions off-shore. The trimaran *Toria* was one of the first to make an impact when she won the first Round Britain Race in 1966. Since that time, both cat and tri racing multi-hulls have dominated the racing scene where all types have raced together, and every open speed record is now held by a multi-hull.

Although these races can be considered as the launching pad of the modern multi-hull movement, they can also be seen as a mixed blessing in the general development of cruising catamarans. The races were responsible for a number of unsuitable multi-hulls, often conceived by inexperienced enthusiasts on shoestring budgets, who then put to sea only to find themselves in difficulties. At the same time the races (such as the transatlantic races organized by the Royal Western Yacht Club (RWYC) in Plymouth) became so popular that the pressure was on every designer and every entrant to produce the ultimate power machine. Each new design had to have more sail area, be lighter in

An early catamaran.

weight and be wider in beam to carry the extra sail. The races were so popular and exciting that they eventually attracted commercial sponsors, particularly from France. The race was on for the ultimate speed machine, but such open rules were bound to amount to a recipe for disaster. Capsizes, craft breaking up and some loss of life were the occasional and not surprising results. Publicity given to such occurrences gave rise to the feeling that multi-hulls in general were subject to capsize and break-up.

Below is a list giving the date of projects and events that influenced the development of non-ballasted sailing boats and lead to the design of the modern catamaran as we know it today:

Trimaran *Toria*.

1945 – Victor Tetchet's trimaran was launched in the US.

1948 – Woody Brown built the 11.9m (39ft) catamaran *Manu Kai*.

1954 – the Prout brothers produced the 4.8m (16ft) 'Shearwater' catamaran. They went on to produce the 8.2m (27ft) 'Ranger' and others.

1955 – James Wharram sailed from the UK to the West Indies in a 7.3m (24ft) catamaran.

1957 – Arthur Piver started to design, build and sail a number of simple plywood trimarans. He sailed extensively in the Pacific and from New York to Plymouth in 1960.

1961 – the 'C' class catamaran was established. Rod MacAlpine-Downie's design won the first 'Little Americas Cup'.

1964 – two catamarans (both with ballast keels) and one trimaran completed the

Prout Power Catamaran.

Single-Handed Transatlantic Race from Plymouth to Newport, Rhode Island.

1966 – the first Round Britain Race was the first race where the multi-hulls dominated the field. Organized by the Royal Western Yacht Club the race runs clockwise around Great Britain, leaving all headlands and off-shore islands (including the Shetlands) to starboard. The 12.8m (42ft) trimaran *Toria* was the easy winner. An invitation to French yachtsman Eric Tabarly to sail *Toria* lead to an explosion of interest in multi-hulls in France. French sponsors, French catamarans and trimarans, and French races have all dominated the open off-shore race scene ever since.

The Modern Multi-Hull

The differences between the racing cat and

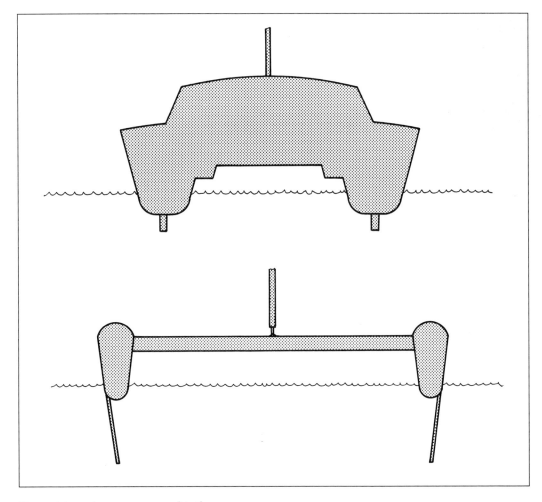

The cruising catamaran compared to the racer.

A Kelly 40 off Brazil.

the cruising cat are now much clearer, so that criticisms of the racing machines are rarely applied to the cruising cats. Top racing catamarans are spidery machines, with long slim hulls, the minimum of beam structure spanning a very wide beam and a towering sailplan, often with a wing mast. The cruiser looks totally different and in no way should it be classified in the same category as the racing craft. With its moderate sailplan, bridge-deck saloon accommodation and being three or four times the weight for the same length, the cruiser operates at a totally different and very much safer level.

The first modern catamarans were often built as one-offs by the owner. The first builders to offer standard designs in glass-reinforced polyester (GRP) began in the mid-1960s. In the UK the production designs available were by Prouts, MacAlpine-Downie, Catalack or Bill O'Brian.

In spite of a certain amount of success for the racing power catamaran and very significant developments for ferries and other commercial uses, the motor yacht is the one area where the catamaran configuration has yet to make an impact. This is because there is not an immediate weight-saving advantage over a ballast keel and hence there is not the same gain in top-speed performance. The justification for the use of the catamaran concept for motor craft is mostly a factor of comfort

A Space 55 off the West Indies.

and space – the prevention of rolling at anchor and the reduction of slamming at speed are both particularly significant benefits. Catamarans also have better fuel efficiency at particular speeds, and I am confident that the motor catamaran is a major trend for the near future.

It was not too many years ago that catamaran skippers met regularly with less than enthusiastic welcomes from marina operators and yacht club committees. Exorbitant extra mooring charges were common. Thankfully, this attitude has been consigned to the history books and the catamaran today is welcomed on a par with other yachts, although some marinas do make an additional charge for the extra beam.

SUMMARY

1662 – Sir William Petty produces cylindrical-hulled catamaran.

1876 – Nathanial Herreshoff design built in the US.

1936 – Eric de Bischop sails catamaran from Hawaii to France.

1945 – Victor Tetchet trimaran launched in the US.

1948 – Woody Brown builds catamaran *Manu Kai*.

1954 – The Prout brothers produce their 'Shearwater' catamaran.

1955 – James Wharram sails a catamaran from the UK to the West Indies.

1957 – Arthur Piver experiments with simple plywood trimarans.

1964 – Catamarans compete in the Single-Handed Transatlantic Race.

1966 – Multi-hulls dominate the first Round Britain Race.

2
WHY A CATAMARAN?

A potential owner will usually base his decision on which yacht to buy on the basis of the following factors: space, performance, comfort, seaworthiness, seakindliness, convenience, appearance, pride of ownership and cost. The order of importance of these factors will differ from person to person. For example, one yacht may be bought for the occasional weekend cruise or even as an alternative to a weekend cottage; another may be for a world cruise lasting several years. In these cases, the first owner's priority may be a low maintenance cost and an appearance that is appealing to his eye. The second owner will certainly be looking for a craft which he can be confident will carry himself and his crew through the most difficult conditions that he is likely to meet.

Catamarans versus Mono-Hulls

When making the comparison with a conventional mono-hull sailing cruiser, the catamaran comes out well – as is seen in the remainder of this section.

Beam

The immediate and most obvious difference

A comparison of the statistics of a typical modern catamaran to a typical mono-hull of the same length.

	34ft Sailing Mono-Hull	Ocean Spirit 34 Catamaran
LOA	10.2m (33.5ft)	10.2m (33.5ft)
LWL	8.5m (27.9ft)	8.8m (28.9ft)
Beam	3.3m (10.8ft)	5.9m (19.4ft)
LWL × Beam	28.1 sq m (301.3 sq ft)	51.9 sq m (560.1 sq ft)
Draft	1.5m (5ft)	0.8m (2.6ft) with fixed keel, 0.6m (2ft) if boards are used.

The LWL × Beam gives an indication of the amount of accommodation, but obviously the actual accommodation space will depend on the style of the yacht. LOA = length overall, LWL = length at water-line.

between mono-hulls and catamarans (*see* table) is the overall beam. At no time when afloat and away from harbour is a wide beam a disadvantage, however, it would be quite wrong to suggest that the extra beam does not present some potential problems to the owner. These might be as listed below:

1.   In the marina. Catamarans are generally too wide for the berths that are designed around traditional width mono-hulls. Fortunately, most marinas have either outside berths where the beam is not a hazard, or shallow water that is unsuitable for deep-keel yachts.

2.   On the slipway. Usually an alternative to slipways can be found – a good example is drying out a catamaran on a beach, which is such a simple matter. Compare this to the use of legs or props which are necessary to hold a mono-hull upright or against a wall.

3.   When too wide for the travel lift.

Many harbours do have cranes available, and it is a good idea for catamaran owners to consider having lifting eyes built in, and to carry their own lifting lines so that it is a simple matter to set up for a crane lift. When it is necessary to work on the hulls or to get at props, a useful idea is to lift one side of the catamaran at a time.

4.   Obviously, moving by road is restricted.

5.   On canals. If your plan is to sail through the French canals to the Mediterranean, your choice of catamaran will be restricted – about 5m (16ft) is the maximum beam on some of the canals.

I believe it is true to say that virtually all catamaran owners accept the above restrictions willingly when they are weighed against the many advantages of the catamaran.

One point to note if you intend to sail through the French canals to the Mediterranean, is that although it is acceptable

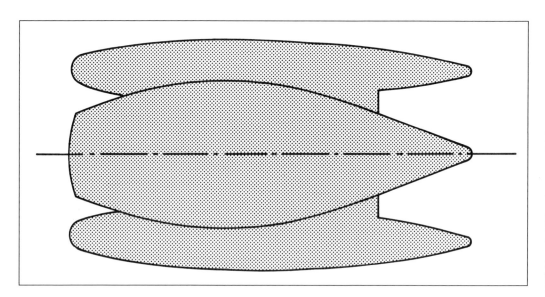

The mono-hull and the catamaran superimposed.

A Solaris Sunrise 36 designed with a 5m (16ft) beam for the French canals, plus her little sister with a 4.3m (14ft) beam.

to choose a narrow-beam catamaran for this purpose, it is not a good idea to choose one as a serious off-shore sailing cruiser on the basis of one trip through the canals.

Efficiency

A distant tall sail heeling to the breeze is a most attractive sight, and few are likely to argue with this. On board, however, the situation is likely to be quite different, one of the major factors in favour of the catamaran exploits just this difference.

The driving power of a sailing yacht is from its sails. The wind pressure acting through the centre of effort of the sails is well above water-level and this induces an overturning moment that has to be resisted by the stability of the floating structure on the water. A single hull with ballast keel heels to the wind pressure, and it is the offset of the weight of the keel from the buoyancy of the hull when heeled that gives the stability. The stability increases with the angle of heel, but initially there is very little stability at low angles of heel.

The situation with a catamaran is quite different. The two hulls are widely spaced and the overturning moment tends to lift one hull and put more weight on to the other. A great deal of stability results from a small change in the angle of heel, the

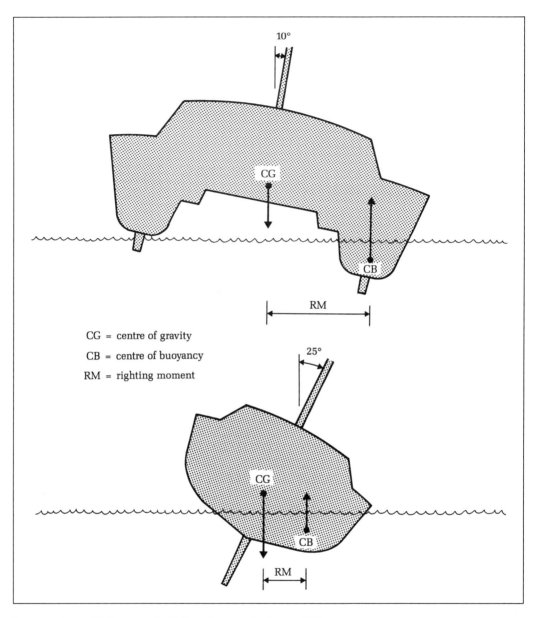

CG = centre of gravity

CB = centre of buoyancy

RM = righting moment

In comparison with the mono-hull, the catamaran heels very little.

catamaran's own weight being sufficient to give the necessary stability. When the extra weight of the ballast in the mono-hull and the difference in the way that stability is gained are taken into account, it is very easy to see that the catamaran configuration is a great deal more efficient.

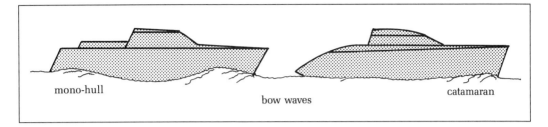

Comparison of bow waves.

The weight factor is most important – the ballast in a mono-hull can constitute as much as 50 per cent of its total weight. The weight is also the starting-point when determining the strength of the structure and all the equipment, hence the need for ballast increases the weight of the whole by more than just the ballast alone. The effect of extra weight and the angle of heel therefore reduce sailing efficiency, but that is still not the end of the story. A mono-hull has more drag when heeled and by necessity, has a wide hull beam. This wide hull beam produces a large bow wave which gives extra resistance and puts a restriction on the maximum speed attainable. This is called the hull speed, and in knots is approximately equal to $1.4 \times \sqrt{\text{the water-line length in feet}}$. As the catamaran has much slimmer hulls, it has no such limit. Heavier cats do have a speed that they achieve with relative ease, but above this they require a lot more drive from the sails.

This very different arrangement of the catamaran therefore creates most of its advantageous features when comparisons are made. These features are: upright sailing, more space, effective accommodation layouts, shallow draft, no fear of running aground, better motion at sea, better performance, ease of handling and so on. Let us look at some of these features in more detail.

Space

The extra accommodation area is perhaps the most immediately obvious advantage and one of the reasons why so many people make the catamaran their choice. Compared with a single-hull craft of the same length, a cat can have as much as twice the space. Looking at the way the accommodation area is laid out with separate, private cabins and a wide, airy saloon further emphasizes the differences between the two. For example, a 13.7m (45ft) catamaran can have four luxury cabins each with own facilities, while a mono-hull would need to be 9m (30ft) or more longer to house the same style of layout.

Comfort, Motion and Upright Sailing

Perhaps the second most prevalent reason for choosing a catamaran is the comfort afforded by the motion of two hulls in waves and the upright sailing situation. Most find life aboard a catamaran much easier than aboard a yacht that regularly heels to angles of 30 degrees or more. While accomplished mono-hull sailors

The saloon of a Maldive 32.

The saloon of a Prout 39.

The saloon of a Space 52.

become quite at ease with the motion of sailing yachts, friends and guests who have not found their sealegs will become ill at ease as soon as the heeling or rolling begins. Catamarans give a much smoother ride, however, and I think it can be said that they have kept many a family together!

A catamaran is relatively light for its overall size and has a lot of buoyancy in its two hulls, the result being that it moves to the pattern of the waves. By contrast, the ballasted single hull acts like a pendulum and has a marked tendency to roll to each wave it meets. The two types have distinctly different motions at sea. When beating to windward, the catamaran has a

quick motion as it meets each wave, while the extra weight of the keel of a single hull slows its reaction time, giving a slower but greater angle of movement. Some find the quicker motion of the catamaran disturbing, but in all other directions of sailing the cat wins every time.

When sailing downwind, the single hull can be most uncomfortable, with the pendulum effect taking over and the boat rolling regularly from side to side. The extreme of this is when the yacht is laid flat in a broach – as seen in spectacular pictures of mono-hull racing in high winds. Most cruisers manage to avoid such extremes, but the rolling is something that mono-hull crews must learn to live with

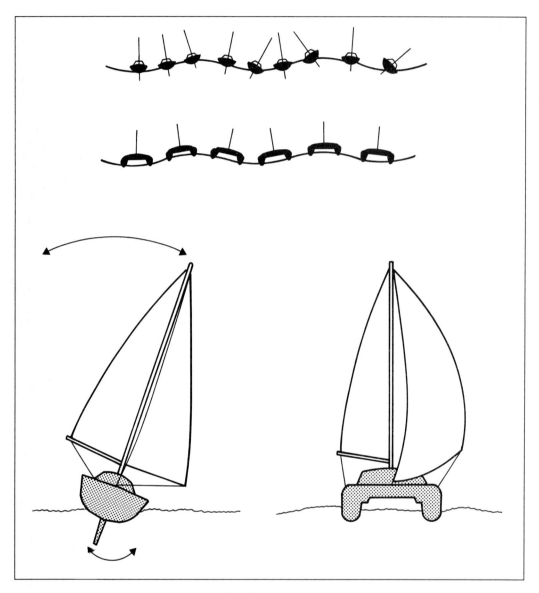

Comparing the effect of waves: the mono-hull suffers from the pendulum effect; the catamaran follows the wave contours.

when sailing downwind. By comparison and in the same conditions, the catamaran crew will enjoy sailing to the full, sliding smoothly down each wave.

When the wind is brisk the catamaran will also surf, doubling its speed for 50m (164ft) or 100m (328ft) stretches at a time. The mainsail is sheeted well out,

Comfort aboard a catamaran – the Kelly 45.

A Sunbeam 24.

downwind headsails are flown and the apparent wind is reduced – all factors contributing to the effect of smooth and easy progress.

Without the steadying effect of the sails, a mono-hull can become most uncomfortable. This might be motoring to windward, lying a-hull to make sail adjustments, lying to a sea-anchor or even lying at anchor in an exposed place. Caught in just the wrong wave pattern, the build-up of the rolling can be quite alarming. In the same circumstances, however, the cat moves to the pattern of the wave, which means that the angle of heel very rarely goes above 10 degrees.

Visible proof of the difference in motion between mono-hulls and catamarans can be seen in the way objects are stowed during a passage. On the mono-hull everything has to be stowed away and strapped down or it will land up on the cabin sole. Aboard the cat, however, most items can be left on tables and the like, and the most that is needed are fiddles around the work surfaces – there is no need for gimballed stoves and so on. I have often heard stories of catamarans, riding out gales, only for the crew to find afterwards that a coffee cup remained on the table throughout.

Handling

The lower weight, the level platform and the easier motion of the catamaran make the handling of sails and the general operation of the boat easier and more suitable for either small crews or even the single-handed yachtsman. Many cats are operated very successfully by husband and wife teams – for more on handling, *see* Chapter 5.

Space for a bath tub.

All-Round View

In marked contrast to the traditional ballasted sailing yacht, the bridge-deck saloon of a catamaran is raised well above the water-line. This allows the saloon to be well ventilated, and allows the crew to be both comfortably seated and have an all-round view. This means that crew members who may not wish or be able to take part in the sailing of the yacht (such as small children or the less agile) are not cut off from the rest of the crew and forced to sit below where they would be unable to see what was happening. Everyone is able to enjoy sailing or just being on board in a way that is not available to those on a

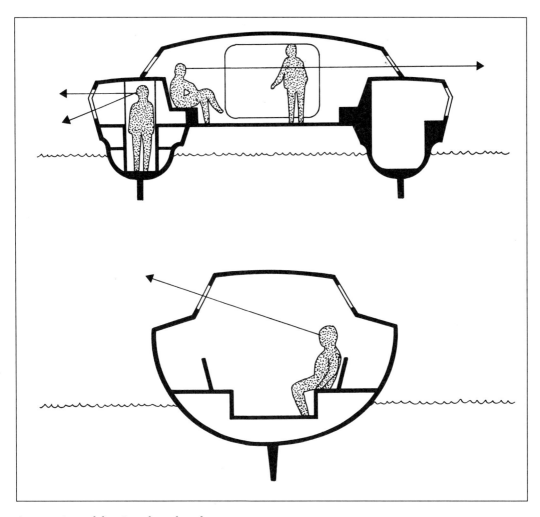

A comparison of the views from the saloons.

mono-hull yacht. However, some cats do fail to make the most of this very important feature – in some instances raised seating may be needed, but this can easily be achieved and a step placed in front of the seat for access. Windows in the cockpit bulkhead and in the door itself can add to the open, spacious atmosphere.

On larger cats designers often try to create the effect of the cockpit being an extension of the saloon, with large patio-style sliding glass doors between the two.

Drying Out at Low Tide

Many of the moorings for boats in the UK are in tidal rivers and estuaries, with boats sitting on the sand or mud at each low tide. As the catamaran settles upright, it is a perfectly reasonable proposition to stop

A day charter catamaran on the beach in Mauritius.

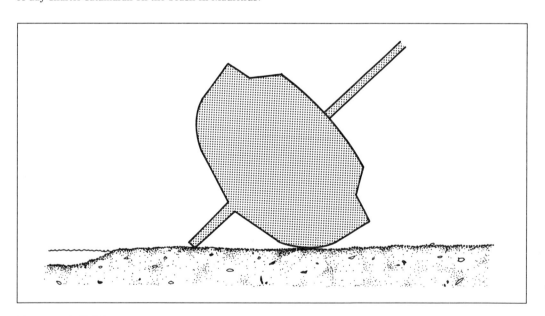

The mono-hull dries out.

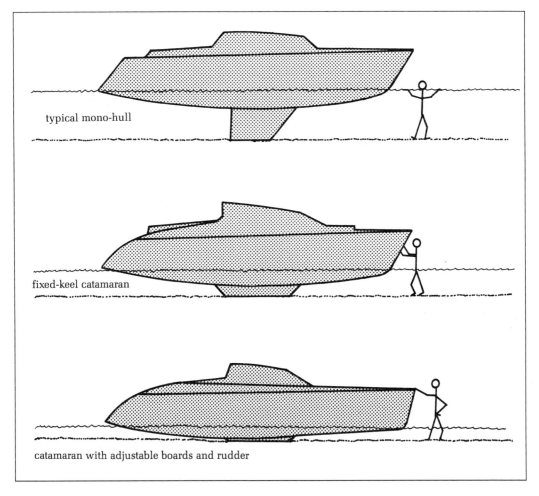

typical mono-hull

fixed-keel catamaran

catamaran with adjustable boards and rudder

Standing alongside in shallow water.

at such a mooring either permanently or just overnight. The crew will be perfectly comfortable and will remain undisturbed as the cat settles – the crew in the average deep-keel mono, however, would be resting at an angle of 45 degrees.

Draft

Most of the production cruising catamarans have shallow, fixed keels but the draft is still usually around 1m (3ft) or less; conventional deep-keel yachts on the other hand have at least a 50 per cent deeper draft. Combined with its light weight, it is therefore perfectly feasible to jump overboard from a cat that has run aground and simply push it back into deep water again. In this way it is also possible to sail safely into or out of very shallow water areas that the deep keeler would have to avoid at all costs. This often includes beating the tide in a tidal river. Running aground with the cat holds no fears, but the same situation on board a mono-hull could easily result in an uncomfortable wait for the next tide at best and real danger at worst.

Sailing Speeds

Being able to get to the next port in the least time is not necessarily of great importance for the true cruising yacht-owner. All owners are proud of their boats, however, and everyone has stories from owners of the most humble of yachts of how they achieved a high average speed or sailed past a particular yacht. Not all cats are fast but they will delight every owner in a good breeze on a reach.

Confidence

In my experience, a newcomer to catamarans can step aboard and immediately feel competent to handle the vessel in normal conditions. This confidence is gained rather more quickly than is the case with a mono-hull of similar size. As experience is gained, the catamaran gives the crew great confidence in its seaworthiness and seakeeping abilities.

Catamarans versus Trimarans

The trimaran is still an option and hence a similar comparison between the catamaran and trimaran is useful.

A major push to the multi-hull movement occurred during the early 1960s. At that time there were a substantial number of catamarans being built, but it was generally the trimaran that was making ocean passages. On a trade-wind crossing I made in 1963 the ratio of tris to cats was in the order of four to one. Today, however, that situation has reversed. Many

---

CATAMARANS VERSUS MONO-HULLS

Catamaran advantages	Catamaran disadvantages
Cannot sink	Can capsize
Space	Storage and handling space
Layout	Is not self-righting
Performance	Quick motion when beating
Reaching and downwind comfort	Bridge-deck slams
Shallow draft	Windage
Dries out when upright	
Beaching	

Mono-hull advantages	Mono-hull disadvantages
Self-righting	Will sink if holed
Regular racing events	Deep draft
Marina space available	Poor space and privacy
	High angles of heel
	Downwind rolling
	Weight
	Pendulum effect

CATAMARANS VERSUS TRIMARANS

Catamaran advantages
Space
Motion on waves
Cost

Catamaran disadvantages
Windward performance
Twin rudders and keels
Twin props

Trimaran advantages
Light air sailing performance
Single rudder and board
Single engine

Trimaran disadvantages
Space
Diagonal stability
Cost of construction
Layout
Storage space
Can dig into waves

---

cruising cats are crossing the oceans and the proportion is now in the order of ten cats for every tri. The early popularity of the trimaran was due to the then wider beam of the tri and to sailors like Arthur Piver who sailed their trimarans across oceans and had their exploits well publicized in yachting magazines.

The modern catamaran has a greater beam to length ratio than its predecessors, and although there are recorded passages of many narrow-beam catamarans, it is the wider beam that gives a much increased sense of security. Other than the space taken in a marina or through canals, there is no real disadvantage to the wider beam.

The angle of heel of a catamaran is dependent on the overall beam. The angle of heel of a trimaran, however, is approximately dependent on the half-beam, or in other words the distance between the two hulls in the water. There is also some extra heel due to the narrower width of the outrigger, which sinks lower in the water under load.

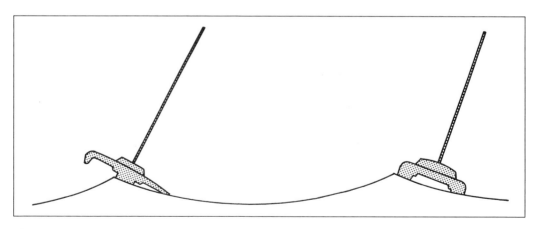

The catamaran versus the trimaran on the wave.

A swing wing trimaran – the Dragonfly.

A modern 9m (30ft) craft – the Sagitta.

Space versus Cost

With the wider beam of today's cats, the stability and the motion aboard is improved, as is the accommodation space. A surprise in the multi-hull's development is that it has not demonstrated a clearly superior performance or a particularly better safety record between cat and tri. This basically leaves you with the choice of the craft with the most amount of space for your money. The three hulls of a trimaran are rather expensive to build, and as the catamaran has a lot more space than a tri it is no surprise that the cat is the first choice for cruising on the basis of space versus cost.

Trimarans in the 6.7–9.1m (22–30ft) range, however, can play quite an interesting role. The larger main hull often has quite good accommodation with good headroom. Various folding methods have also been devised for some designs to reduce the beam when the trimaran is being towed or when it is in a marina. It is also quite difficult to style a bridge-deck saloon catamaran in this size range effectively with even sitting headroom. Trimarans of this size can have good performance, but they do tend to be rather more expensive to produce than the equivalent mono-hull or catamaran.

There are larger trimarans where the accommodation area is carried right across and into the outriggers. These compete on space with the cats, but are still more costly to build.

A modern 9m (30ft) craft – the Suncat.

Motion

The way in which the trimaran acts in wind and sea is the one area in which it has a following. The trimaran reacts to the wind and waves in a more responsive manner than the catamaran. It heels with the wind and reacts to each wave, giving a feeling that is more akin to that felt in a dinghy or keel yacht.

SUMMARY

- The overall beam of a catamaran can cause some difficulties in the marina or harbour, or on canals or whilst in road transit, but when afloat and away from harbour the wide beam causes no problems.

- Compared with a mono-hull, a catamaran offers a great deal more accommodation space, a smoother motion at sea and, with a shallow draft, no fear of running aground.

- Catamarans can often be operated successfully with only a two-person crew.

- When choosing for cruising, the catamaran has a lot more space than the trimaran, and is, as a consequence, better value for money.

- For the newcomer, the catamaran offers the chance of greater confidence on the water than would a mono-hull.

3

CATAMARAN TYPES
AND FEATURES

A single-hulled yacht has a certain shape and a beam to length ratio which vary relatively little from one model to the next. These factors determine the volume of a particular length of yacht, and hence the accommodation of one 9m (30ft) yacht cannot vary too much from that of any other yacht of the same length. By comparison, the catamaran configuration offers the designer a wide variety of hull beam to length ratios, overall beam to length ratios, styles and layouts. At one extreme you can have just two slim hulls and a beam connection, and at the other extreme you can have full-length beam cabins and saloon. The amount of interior volume is a major factor in determining the final weight, and putting this weight with the rig and engine choice determines the performance style of the catamaran.

With such variation to consider, I have attempted to list the categories that cover the options:

1. The open bridge-deck catamaran. This style will often be demountable or trailable at the smaller sizes (under 9m or 30ft), but can be of any size. Most designers have such models in their portfolios, which can be either cruisers or racers. With a minimal structure the

weight should be low and performance good, but this is not always the case.
2. The cruising/racing catamaran. These cats will usually have a relatively small bridge-deck saloon and open areas between the hulls fore and aft. They also have a simple layout and a specification with a tall rig for good performance.
3. The strictly cruising or live-aboard catamaran. This catamaran style will make maximum use of the space available, and will preferably be designed with plenty of extra buoyancy to carry all the cruising gear and stores most serious cruisers like to carry. Some designs fall short in this allowance and tend to become overloaded when setting off for a long cruise. The majority of production cats fall into this category to appeal to the family.
4. Motor-sailing catamaran. The traditional motor-sailer mono-hull is a heavy, comfortable yacht but has limitations on performance under both power and sail. The catamaran offers the chance to have the best of both worlds with less of a compromise on performance. The lack of a hull speed limitation is the prime reason for this – increasing the power of the engines will increase the speed. The power required goes up as the square of the speed so extra weight and fuel are carried but, within reasonable limits,

Open bridge-deck type – the Tini 27.

Open bridge-deck on a 12m (39ft) craft.

these can be carried without unduly compromising the sailing speeds, depending on the particular style, size and design. The windage of the rig is an obvious limiting factor in terms of the practical top speed under power.

At the top end of this type are examples of fast sailing cats which have engines producing over 20 knots. For those in a hurry, there is no better alternative, and any cat powered for a speed of 12 knots or more would fall into this category.

5. Day and cabin charter cats. Catamarans are used extensively for charter work with considerable success. The space and low angle of heel are the attractions to the charter customer. The dedicated day charter cat is designed to carry the maximum number of passengers on deck and often in a specially designed

A fast cruiser – the Suncat 40.

open-style saloon. The typical luxury cabin charter-style catamaran will have accommodation for four or five couples, each having their own facilities.

Obviously, there are no distinct lines between each category. Also worth a mention here is an extension of the cruising/racing category. We have seen how a catamaran can house more cabins and carry more home comforts than the equivalent mono-hull, however, some owners want a larger yacht for its general performance and seakindliness but do not need a large crew or more cabins. Such a specification gives the designer the scope to produce an extremely attractive vessel, with sparkling performance and very comfortable accommodation for a small crew. Such cats have the ability to cross oceans at speeds approaching those of the dedicated racing machines and offer the most enjoyable sailing of all. Such an owner who wants to sail fast but needs less in the way of space and home comforts will find a number of cat designs from which to choose, offered by custom catamaran builders. These cats need not necessarily have very large rigs – they are light in weight and have easily driven hulls, so that a modest sailplan which is easily handled by a small crew will drive the cat at high speed in complete safety. This is catamaran sailing at its best.

Designed for accommodation – the Heavenly Twins.

Hulls

Hull Shapes

Most standard production catamarans have simple round bilge hulls for least wetted surface and best efficiency. For production in GRP the compound curvature does not present a problem or add to the cost after the initial work on the moulds has been carried out.

Asymmetric hulls have been tried in an attempt to eliminate the need for appendages for lateral resistance, but the experiments were of only limited success and such hulls are rarely seen today. Deep, narrow 'V' hulls are another approach to

the same problem. Such designs are reasonably effective and relatively easy to build as one-offs, but obviously the accommodation area is restricted within the narrow hulls and there is also increased drag due to the extra wetted surface.

Hard chine hulls are usually chosen out of simplicity for one-off building. Such hulls are usually made of four or five panels. For cruising catamarans there is relatively little difference in performance between the hard chine hull and round bilge hull. Probably the only objection to the hard chine hull is its appearance – the round bilge tends to have the more professional look.

Another style of hull uses a flare or

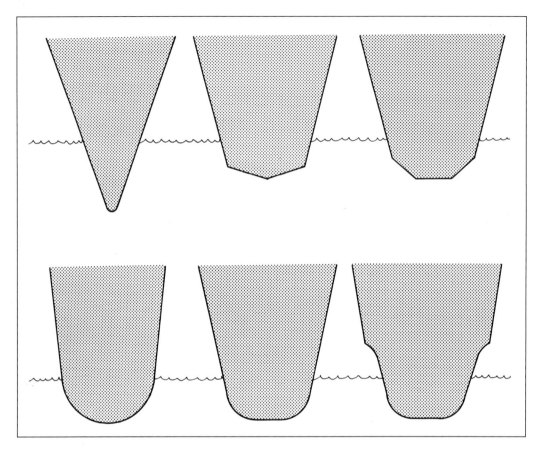

Hull sections.

knuckle to increase the hull width above the water-line. This is an elegant way of increasing the in-hull space most effectively, and is used to give the width for a double bunk in an otherwise narrow hull.

The top-sides of catamaran hulls are reasonably flat compared to the usual compound curvature of a mono-hull. Some designs keep the top sides close to to upright, while other designs angle the top side out at angles of up to 20 or 25 degrees. Appearance, side-deck width and ease of building are the usual reasons for this choice, but there is little other difference

in terms of normal sailing. Should the windward hull lift high, the angled side has the effect of moving the centre of buoyancy to give a slightly better chance of recovery.

Overhangs at the bow and stern are decided on questions of efficiency and styling – any yacht should be pleasing to the eye. As a raked stem and a long overhanging counter add style to a traditional yacht's appearance, so too does the same apply to the catamaran. Unfortunately, however, overhangs do little for a catamaran's performance, and if you are looking for the best results from a certain overall length you have to compromise.

Plumb Stems

Performance is a function of water-line length and has resulted in the plumb stem being used on many craft – not only on catamarans – and some would say that this is to the detriment of the boat's appearance. The difference its use has on performance for a cruiser is very small, but it has a greater effect on smaller sized craft than on larger ones – on the latter a 1 per cent improvement in performance is probably a reasonable figure. As there are many other factors which affect the craft's performance to a similar degree, style should not be unduly compromised to achieve maximum length on the water-line.

There has been some discussion as to whether the plumb stem will contribute to a pitchpole-style capsize by reducing the reserve buoyancy at the bow. The answer here depends on how the designer achieves the plumb stem. If the designer draws the usual underwater shape and then simply cuts back the usual bow overhang, the reserve buoyancy obviously is reduced. If, on the other hand, the designer draws the usual deck length and then extends the water-line to give a finer entry, he actually increases the reserve buoyancy slightly. The important factor here is the relationship between the centre of gravity and the reserve buoyancy.

Bow Bulbs

Bow bulbs have been used on a number of craft and, as a result, various claims for

The bow bulb on a South African Deancat.

improved performance have been made. It should also be pointed out, however, that bulbs have appeared on some designs only to disappear on the next year's model. The truth is probably that any difference is not really noticeable. In my view it is an area where further experimentation is needed, but the potential gains are always going to be relatively small for the cruiser.

Appendages

Keels, trim boards and rudders are additions to the hull which are used to affect balance, lateral resistance, directional stability and steering control.

KEELS
Keels provide lateral resistance to reduce leeway when sailing to windward and to give directional control. A good cruising catamaran can be expected to sail to windward with an apparent wind angle of 35 or 40 degrees, to have a leeway angle of 4 or 5 degrees and to make good

approximately 45 or 50 degrees to the true wind.

A deep, high-aspect ratio board or keel is the most effective for control and for windward ability, and can be found on racing craft. A cruising cat's windward ability is of slightly less concern and therefore a compromise is the usual solution. The keels can be fixed, a single board in one hull, twin boards in both hulls or a single board from the bridge-deck between the hulls can be used. It is probably true to say, that 95 per cent of all cats are now built with fixed keels, in that they are simpler to build and have no moving parts. Against these advantages is the disadvantage of additional fixed draft – usually 30–45cm (1–1½ft). Also, the fixed keel does go against the theory that in a storm it would be better if the boat can be allowed to slide sideways in a broach or lying a-hull.

The movable boards that can be used are the daggerboard type or the pivoting centre-board type. The latter have the advantage of being able to swing back in the

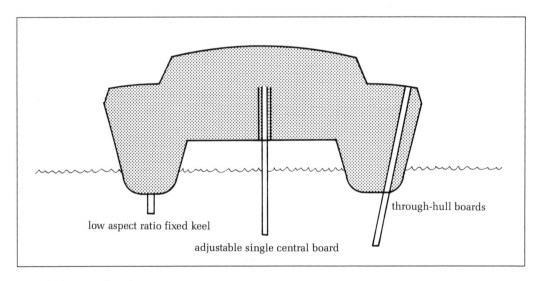

low aspect ratio fixed keel

adjustable single central board

through-hull boards

Fixed keels versus boards.

event of collision, but they usually take up more space, require a long slot in the hull and are more difficult to construct. Catamarans with daggerboards in their hulls usually have some form of crash box, but still take the risk of more serious damage in the event of a collision at high speed. A single board in one hull only is quite effective, with little or no noticeable difference on opposite tacks. This is used for simplicity and to save space.

The attraction of a single board on the centreline from the bridge-deck is that the chance of damage is limited to the area above water-level. It can often be arranged between bunks on the bridge-deck and hence takes no space away from the accommodation. The single central board is usually used with a single central rudder. In this way the cat has a minimum fixed draft for creeping into knee-deep water, and appendages that are very simply raised and lowered.

A single rudder – easily adjusted in shallow water.

TRIM BOARDS

As a general rule, any board arrangement does give less directional stability than the fixed keel equivalent. To counter this I suggest the use of trim boards that can easily be arranged in the transom steps aft. The trim boards are daggerboard-style and of a similar size to the rudders. In practice when down, the trim boards, only slightly hinder steering, but they do reduce the steering effort considerably, particularly in high winds and waves when running.

RUDDERS

The most common rudder system now to accompany the usual fixed keel arrangement is twin spade rudders mounted on stainless steel stern tube stocks which are permanently fixed in the hulls. The rudder depth should be slightly less than the keels, and there should be some balance to reduce steering loads – the ideal is approximately 17 per cent of the area ahead of the pivot line. A skeg ahead of the rudder works well, but it does eliminate the balance and is not as easy to build as the spade-type rudder. It is often used as a way of protecting the rudder, but it is a simple matter to make a spade rudder strong enough without the need for such a skeg – strong enough in fact to take the weight of the aft end of the boat.

Where the object is to maintain minimum draft, rudders need to be designed so that they can be lifted, but preferably with the ability to steer the boat at an intermediate depth. However, other than with the single rudder mentioned above, this is not an easy matter to arrange.

A single rudder and trim boards on a 12m (40ft) boat.

Steering

A common arrangement for steering with twin rudders is to use a connecting bar between the tillers, placed either above deck level or hidden within the structure. The former is the simplest method, but it creates a hazard to anyone standing near the tillers as they sweep the aft deck. With this arrangement the steering can be direct tiller steering, although it can be difficult to arrange the tillers so that the helmsman has a good view over the bridge-deck saloon. It is for this reason that most cats are fitted with wheel steering.

Where a direct connection between tillers is not practical, it is quite common to have separate systems to each rudder from a single wheel. The steering system can be operated either by cable or hydraulically. Hydraulic steering has proved to be effective on all sizes, although there does tend to be a loss of feedback and hence a loss of feel. On the other hand, hydraulic steering is perhaps the easiest system to which an autopilot or power steering can be added.

Autopilots

Autopilots have developed to the stage where they are both reliable and inexpensive. The autopilot can be attached to a tiller or the wheel, or through the hydraulic system.

Wind-vane steering has not been

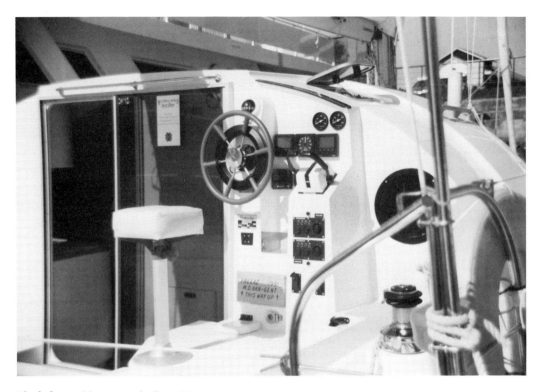

The helm position on an Antigua 37.

particularly successful on fast catamarans due to the rates of acceleration of these lightweight craft. They are also much more costly than electronic pilots.

Helm Positions

The majority of catamarans have the helm position set against the cockpit bulkhead. The helmsman has a view over the saloon, he is close to sheet winches on the coach-roof and he is at least partly protected from wind and spray from ahead. A few cats have twin wheels so that the person at the helm can be on the windward side – or on the sunny side if it is a nice day.

A few of the French catamarans have T-shaped cockpits, with a wheel in each aft corner. This gives the helmsman or woman an excellent view of the sails and can be very practical in favourable weather, but it is not as attractive an arrangement in inclement conditions.

Some larger cats have a raised helm position, where the wheel and all sheet winches are arranged around an opening in the coachroof. Even larger cats can have a flying-bridge-style helm above the level of the top of the saloon.

The Interior

Headroom

Where there is a saloon, even the fairly

The raised helm position on a Space 52.

The Elf 26 – an example of tiller steering.

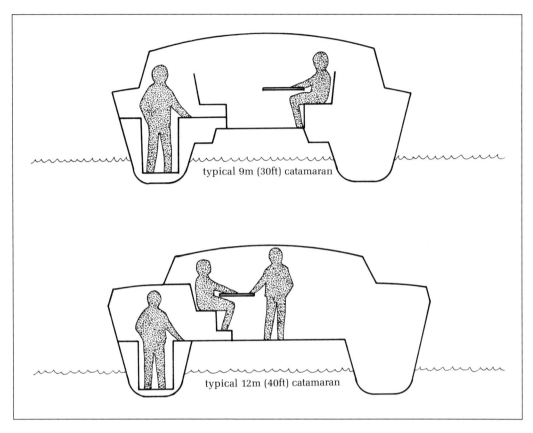

typical 9m (30ft) catamaran

typical 12m (40ft) catamaran

Headroom on two typical catamarans.

small catamarans will have standing headroom in the hulls. This is produced by carrying the coachroof sufficiently far over the hull, but leaving a narrow side-deck so that people can walk past the coachroof on the outside. Some side-decks are, however, very narrow.

In much larger catamarans there is headroom within the hulls below the sheer. This can be provided for at an intermediate size, but doing so usually puts the deck at an awkwardly high level at the bow when coming into a marina.

Another practical approach when creating headroom is to have a raised level from the deck edge. This has the advantage of wide side-decks and decks at a convenient height at the bow and stern.

Saloon standing headroom is usual in catamarans which have an overall length of about 10.7m (35ft) and over. In catamarans below this length, the saloon will usually have sitting headroom only.

The Bridge-Deck

Nacelle

Nacelle is the term used for the lowering

Nacelles on an Event 34.

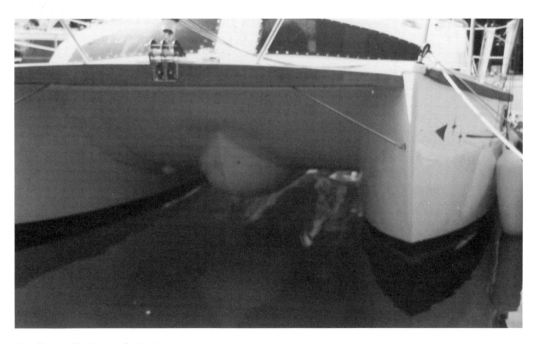

Nacelles on the Heavenly Twins.

Nacelles on a Sunrise 36.

and shaping of a section of the bridge deck along the centreline. It is employed for a number of reasons, particularly in some 9–12m (30–40ft) boats. In the saloon it may add useful headroom just inside the door, thus reducing the height of the coachroof. By running the nacelle aft into the cockpit there is a convenient engine mounting arrangement when using a sonic leg. The nacelle can also be used to support a single board and single rudder.

The nacelle can be quite close to the water without suffering unduly from slamming, depending on its shape and position fore and aft. It is obviously preferable to have a nacelle and step in the bridge-deck rather than lowering the whole of the bridge-deck. The nacelle and step have the effect of breaking up any waves that hit the underside of the bridge-deck and reducing the resulting impact. It will also stiffen the structure. A large nacelle and low bridge-deck clearance may, however, have the effect of limiting higher speeds due to the build-up of bow waves and spray between the water and the nacelle bridge-deck assembly.

On similar lines, a step in the bridge-deck beside the hull can add some very useful space. It can be designed at the level of the bunks to turn a single into a double, or make it possible to fit the berths across the hull. This step becomes the first step down from saloon to hull.

Bridge-Deck Clearance

Both the clearance between the water and bridge-deck and the length of the bridge-deck have an important effect on both performance and slamming. Unless the bridge-deck is exceptionally high, the catamarans will slam from time to time. This is often no more than the bang of the wave as it hits, with no other ill-effect. However, there are catamarans with low bridge-deck clearance that suffer from slamming when they are beating to windward in waves. Usually no harm is done other than a reduction in speed. Some designs also suffer from a speed-limiting situation that can be most frustrating – this occurs when sailing downwind at speed with the result that the water boils up between the hulls. It is similar to the feeling that the brakes have been applied, just when the best and most exhilarating sailing would otherwise have been the case if there was more clearance. Obviously, the longer and lower the bridge-deck and the more heavily loaded it is, the more severe the problem. Due to wave interaction between the hulls, the worst slamming tends to be somewhere under the mast area and again under the cockpit. Some designs reduce the potential to slam by raising the bridge-deck except in the area where the headroom is needed most – in other words, just inside the saloon. Wider beam catamaran designs need greater bridge-deck clearance than narrow beam cats if they are to avoid slamming.

Slamming is one of the most common criticisms of some catamarans. This is the reason that most of the newer designs are tending towards higher bridge-deck clearance, and accepting more windage and a

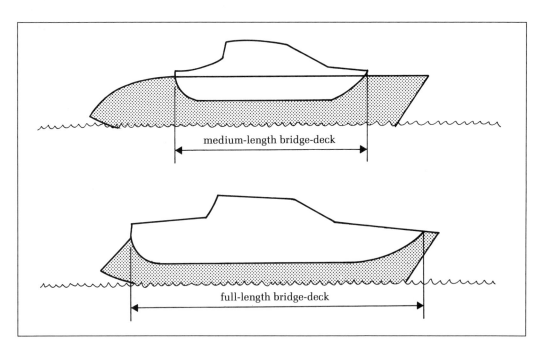

Bridge-deck length and clearance.

higher profile. There is the theory that cats with very low bridge-deck clearance will slam with less severity. Obviously this is true – if you stand very close to someone you cannot hit them with any force. When this is put into practice, however, it results in the problem of reduced performance due to wave interference and drag.

Length of Bridge-Deck

On the question of slamming, the length of the bridge-deck structure is just as important as the clearance. A short length of bridge-deck, with low clearance in the right places fore and aft can be quite free of slamming.

There is considerable variation between the lengths of the solid bridge-deck between different designs. The most

accommodation-oriented cats will be decked from bow to stern, while others will have an open area at both the bow and stern. An open area aft makes a convenient place to carry the tender on davits or other lifting mechanism without extending beyond the length of the boat. Forward, the open area is usually fitted with a net or trampoline – a good place for sunbathing.

The design with the least bridge-deck structure is likely to have less weight and to be the best boat in terms of sailing. In a storm, the more open decking is likely to be most seaworthy with less deck on which the water can have an effect. This is another typical compromise for the catamaran designer, bearing in mind that for the majority of the time that a catamaran is being used as a cruiser, a lot of solid decking to walk on is an asset.

Transom steps on the Privilege.

Transom steps on an Antigua 37.

Transom steps on the Kelly 42.

Other Features

Transom Steps

Transom steps are a feature that should be on all cats. Whether getting aboard from a marina, a dinghy or the water, this is the easiest way. The steps are also a popular place to sit while sailing as they are close to the water and provide a comfortable seat away from the rest of the crew. The safety rails should be designed to suit.

Mast Step

Depending on the accommodation design

Escale 39 – the latest Prout.

Wing mast stepped at deck level.

Mast on a coachroof.

and the rig chosen, the mast will be stepped on the coachroof, or just foward of the saloon at deck level, for easier operation of halyards. If stepped on the coachroof, a mast support is needed inside and some structure to take the load below.

Lifelines

Catamarans should have stanchions and lifelines all round – just like any other yacht. Although the cat does not heel it can move rapidly and cause unsuspecting members of crew to lose their footing. The forward pulpits are a favourite place to sit and watch the waves go by, and some

builders incorporate a seat into it. The usual way to get aboard is via transom steps – a gate aft is needed in the lifelines if best use is to be made of this access.

A safety line from the cockpit to the bow can very easily be arranged aboard a cat. In severe conditions a member of the crew can hook his or her safety harness onto the safety line and move about without much danger.

Tankage

Most catamarans do not have enough space below the floorboards for tanks in the hulls. The alternatives are to position them under bunks in the hulls, in units in

Trampoline life-lines all round on a Privilege.

the hulls or on the bridge-deck. The latter is a compromise in that it is preferable for the weight to be as low as possible. However, as the vertical position of the weight does not have any great effect until a high angle of heel is reached, this is acceptable. The fuel will often be in the structure aft of the cockpit and the water in the saloon seating or just forward. It is not good practice to have heavy items in the bows.

It is important that the tanks are easily reached and have inspection hatches that allow access to all parts of the tank and fittings. Long shallow tanks should therefore be avoided. Petrol tanks and gas bottles should be stowed in self-draining compartments – these are easy to arrange on the bridge-deck of the catamaran.

Instruments

Catamarans do not differ in their requirements and should be fitted with all the usual instruments – speed, wind, depth and positioning instruments, and radar, radio and so on. There is a vast choice and new instruments available every year. The radar scanner should be mounted on the mast at first spreader level, or on a special post aft.

SUMMARY

- The open bridge-deck catamaran has the least structure, resulting in a low weight and good performance.

- Cruising/racing catamarans offer a simple layout and specification with a tall rig for good performance.

- For the family, strictly cruising or live-aboard catamarans offer the maximum usage of space available and extra buoyancy, making them ideal for long cruises.

- The motor-sailing catamaran offers comfort with less performance compromise than the traditional motor-sail mono-hull.

- For the charter customer, catamarans offer space and a low angle of heel. Luxury charter catamarans can accommodate four or five couples, each having their own facilities.

4
RIGS AND ENGINES

Catamaran Rigs

The wide base of the catamaran has obvious advantages when it comes to both supporting the mast and sheeting in the sails, but in all other ways the rig has the same job to do and is very similar to that on any other sailing yacht.

The forestay fitting falls between the two bows and is usually supported on the deck structure or on a beam between the two bows. To take the load on the middle of the beam, there will usually be a bridle over a strut from the forestay fitting.

Taking the main shrouds to the deck edge has the effect of reducing the compression in the mast and the stress in the stay, but the extra stability of the catamaran does mean that the rig can be subject to greater loads than the mono-hull which heels to the wind. The result is that most catamarans have the same or slightly heavier mast sections and rigging than a mono-hull of the same length. However, not all catamarans use the full width for the shrouds and instead use a mono-hull-style rigging plan on a narrow base. The latter arrangement allows for a large overlapping Genoa.

Virtually every type of rig has been used on catamarans – from Chinese junk rigs to solid wings. Each have advantages and disadvantages. As with all aspects of design, it is a question of which compromise is best suited to the particular application.

Full Roach Main ¾ Rig

Currently, the most common rig used in new designs is the fractional ¾ or ⅞ rig with relatively small Genoa and full roach battened main. As a larger version of the day catamaran such as the Hobiecat, this can be on a rotating or a fixed mast. It is an efficient sailplan that makes good use of the wide base for the stays, and which puts least stress on the structure or the spars themselves. The small Genoa requires

A Tini 27 in Mauritius. It has a ¾ rig with just three mainstays, forestay and shrouds.

55

less winch grinding when tacking and the mainsail, once it is raised, is relatively easy to control. The large roach mainsail dictates that there can be no fixed backstays.

The basic plan has shrouds that are angled aft. The forestay is kept tight by using the mainsheet tackle or, more effectively, by using a runner from the hound position. Some may suggest that running backstays are not to be recommended on cruising boats, but I should point out that they are operated in a different way to the backstays usually found on mono-hulls. The runners are widely spaced so that adjustment is not essential when beating to windward. Also, they are there to tighten the forestay only and will usually pose no danger to the rig if they are not operated correctly.

It is also suggested by some that this mast, which is supported from only one point by just three stays, is in some way likely to be more prone to failure. I do not see this as a problem as any rig will fail if any of the stays fails while it is under tension.

The biggest rigging load on any rig is on the forestay, in order to keep the stay reasonably straight. Of course, this has to be balanced by backstay loads which together induce compression in the mast. Anything that is done to reduce the forestay load, such as reducing its length with ¾ rig, reduces the loads in all parts of the rig. A diamond stay arrangement will usually be used between the hounds and the foot of the mast. Another feature I like with this arrangement is that it does not require the rigging to be set up tight and therefore avoids building stresses into the rig.

Using the ¾ or ⅞ rig makes it a relatively simple matter to use a rotating mast or small wing mast. Rotating masts are not common on cruising catamarans, but there are a few and the owners are very pleased with the extra efficiency achieved.

The large roach main is usually slab reefed, but the new in-boom roller systems do cater for the fully battened sail. The full-length battens also have the advantage of stopping the sail flogging in very strong winds when either reefing or raising the sail.

Masthead Rig

The conventional masthead rig that is seen on a majority of cruising mono-hulls is the next most likely choice for catamarans. Some are rigged in mono-hull style on a narrow base to leave room for the overlapping Genoa outside the rigging; others make use of the full-width staying base by having a masthead shroud to the deck edge and diamonds to stiffen the mast between masthead and foot. The shroud may be set slightly aft of the mast to allow a larger overlap of the Genoa. Any restriction on the Genoa overlap is not a major loss on a catamaran as the very large overlap seen on many mono-hulls is actually relatively inefficient on a catamaran.

The mainsail has a smaller roach than the fractional rig, eliminating the weight and cost of full-length battens and making it easier to raise and lower the sail.

Mast Aft Rig

Due to the use of the mast aft rig by Britain's most successful cat producer, Prout Catamarans, this rig can be seen in most UK harbours. It has the advantage that the halyards are operated from the cockpit and that the largest sail, the

An Event with its mast on cockpit bulkhead.

A Space 55 – an older ketch.

Genoa, is rolled away and reefed on its headsail roller gear. The very small mainsail is obviously also easy to handle. Other claims are made for the lifting effect of the large Genoa at the bow. The trade-off for this, however, is the effort required to sheet the large Genoa at each tack and the fact that the long forestay is not well supported by the backstays. It is also difficult to achieve the desirable tight forestay for best windward performance.

Ketch and Cutter Rig

Many of the larger cruisers use ketch or cutter rigs to reduce the size of individual sails, and so that the balance of the sailplan can be adjusted – in other words, the main of the ketch can be lowered, or the main reefed and the yankee dropped on a cutter and the sail balance retained. Both ketch and cutter rigs have been used on cats but there is some loss of efficiency, particularly on the faster boats. It can be particularly difficult to get a yankee, and staysail and main working together on the faster cutter catamaran. With the ketch, the mizzen is relatively ineffective both running and hard on the wind, hence it is hard to justify the extra cost and complication of a mizzen mast. Where many cats do have a staysail, it is very often used just as a storm sail and is rolled away in favour of a conventional Genoa in lighter winds.

One point in favour of the ketch rig is the mizzen staysail which is an attractive sail to use on a reach. The mizzen mast is also a good place for the radar mounting.

A Tango 52 with cutter headsails.

Side-by-Side Masts

Just about every possible configuration of hulls and rigs has been put to the test over recent years. If we have two hulls, why not two rigs? There have been a number of examples of these, but with limited success. There are some interesting possibilities for simple sail handling and a low centre of effort, but this set-up will not be adopted generally.

Unstayed Masts

There are a number of very successful cruising mono-hulls that have unstayed masts. Again, there are some interesting possibilities for catamarans, particularly with their advantage of the wide deck for

sheeting. Eliminating rigging drag and using a rotating wing section would be very effective, but its use will probably be limited to experimental sailors.

Other Rigs

Junk, Spritsail, Gunther and so on, and even the crab-claw have all been tried but not in sufficient numbers to warrant any detailed discussion here.

Sails

Most cats come with a mainsail, a Genoa and a storm jib or staysail. For light winds there is the choice of either spinnakers or cruising chutes. The catamaran has a great advantage in having the extra width on which to sheet the running sails – a spinnaker can be flown without a spinnaker pole, making setting, sheeting and dousing the sail a lot simpler. A favourite sail for many cat owners is the cruising chute, which is similar to a spinnaker but asymmetric. It is tacked to the bow with a single sheet to the clew. It has less area than a spinnaker but can be carried much closer to the wind. I find it preferable to have two or three cruising chutes for different conditions and wind speeds than to have spinnakers.

Some years ago it was common practice for long-distance cruisers to have twin Genoas for self-steering, but with the advent of simple electronic steering equipment and battery charging, the need for other steering systems is no longer relevant for most.

Reefing

Headsail rollers are standard on practically

A Tiki 36 – the sails wrap around the mast to form a wing.

Roller gear on a Privilege.

all yachts for both reefing and stowing. Few sails are particularly efficient when well reefed this way, but this is a compromise the cruising yachtsman is happy to accept in order to avoid the task of changing sails on the foredeck.

The simplest and easiest to handle is mainsail reefing inside or behind the mast. It is very similar to the Genoa roller in operation. In this case the sail cannot have battens and hence has to have a straight leach. Some sail area is lost as a consequence which is particularly detrimental to light wind performance, and there is also some extra weight aloft in the heavier mast section.

Where a sail is rolled around a stay there is always a chance that problems can

A slab-reefed main and roller-reefed Genoa.

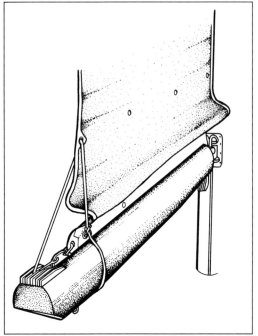

Slab reefing.

occur. Current gear is well tried and tested but there is still the occasional incident where the sail unrolls in a gale or when it will not roll up as required.

The options for reefing the full roach, fully battened main lie between slab reefing and one of the newer systems for rolling around the boom or in the boom. Rolling around the boom is not new but was rarely satisfactory for reefing as the sail tends to roll unevenly and bunch at the mast. The new systems use a very small luff rope in place of the slides and have the pivot for the boom forward of the line of the luff so that there should be no build-up at the front end. The boom has to be kept at right angles to the mast while rolling. The advantage of the system is that it results in a neatly stowed sail within the boom and no separate sail cover is needed.

Sailtainer – one of a number of in-boom roller systems.

Three-way diamonds on a Privilege.

A Kelly 45 – the spinnaker is flown without a pole.

Slab reefing involves a hook at the luff and a line to the leach, threaded through the boom, or lines to both that have the effect of pulling down a slab of the sail to the boom. This is a relatively simple operation and is the first choice for most cat owners. It is still necessary to get to the boom and tie up the excess sail area. A loose-footed mainsail is commonly used.

Lazy jacks are lines from the mast that catch the sail as it is lowered. However, they are a mixed blessing as they tend to get caught in the battens when raising the sail unless some provision is made to pull them out of the way. Some systems combine lazy jacks with the sail cover to 'catch' the sail on the boom.

Auxiliary Engines

Outboards

A high proportion of smaller catamarans use an outboard motor as their auxiliary. Anyone who has a long association with multi-hulls will have memories of the frustration of dealing with temperamental outboards. Fortunately, today's outboards with their solid-state electrics are far more reliable than they were just a few years ago, and hence outboards are a practical and economical answer to the auxiliary question. This is particularly so with the availability of four-stroke engines designed for better thrust at slower speeds.

The cat configuration overcomes most

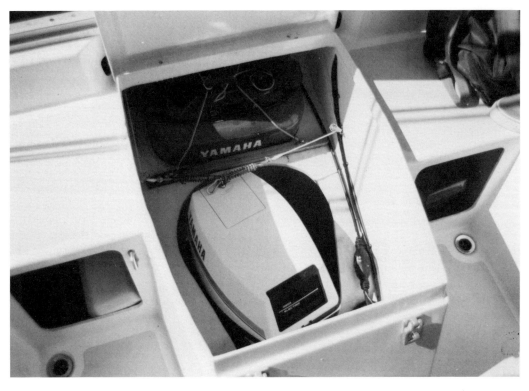

The outboard in the cockpit seat of a Sunbeam. Note the connection to the steering cables.

of the objection to the hazard of petrol on board. Both the outboard and the tank can be arranged in such a way that any leaks or spillage immediately drain overboard and not into the bilges. Most designers make special provision for the outboard, perhaps mounting it in a nacelle or, if twin outboards are used, under cockpit seats, so that the outboard only requires tilting to put it into operation. The inconvenience of having outboards on lifting brackets hung over the transom is mostly a thing of the past, except in the case of very small cats.

A point to consider is that a catamaran has quite a lot of windage and relatively little of the boat is in the water. The effect is that the wind can make controlling a cat in windy conditions and in close quarters quite a difficult task. The best solution is to have twin propellers. Twin propellers set at the hull spacing give excellent control – the cat can be turned on the spot. Twin outboards (usually set under cockpit seats) are a valid solution and are the first choice for economy, least weight and best control. They have been used most successfully on cats up to 12m (40ft) and more.

The 9.9 Yamaha outboard motor is a good engine to consider as it has a large, slow-turning propeller that is very effective at the speed required of an auxiliary. Where twins are fitted it is quite practical and efficient to use just one engine until the other is needed for a manoeuvre, and using this technique you basically have the reliability of two totally independent units.

Effective diesel outboards are also available now. They are not cheap or particularly light in weight by comparison, but they do have the advantages of being simple to install and remove for maintenance, and the prop is out of the water when not in use.

Diesel Engines

It is traditional for well-equipped cruising yachts to have diesel engines. The cat is no different in this respect, except that one could argue that fitting two diesels to an efficient sailing craft is rather excessive.

The question is whether to use one or two diesels, and whether to have the props in the water. Every possible combination of legs, saildrives, standard stern tubes and hydraulic drives has been used, with fixed, folding or controllable pitch props – the extra speed of the catamaran increases the incentive to reduce the drag of a fixed prop in the water when sailing.

The most common catamaran diesel installation is twin saildrives or the single engine, mounted in a central nacelle in the cockpit area with a sonic cat leg drive. The saildrive is effective, but it does often either take up valuable cabin space or has to be fitted under a raised bunk. A few owners have fitted one saildrive in one hull and reported that they were entirely satisfied with the installation. I am sure that this arrangement can cope with most conditions, but it must be lacking on some occasions.

A sonic catamaran leg from the diesel inboard on an Event 34.

The sonic cat leg is produced by Sillete Ltd specially for catamarans. There are obvious advantages: the engine is away from the accommodation, the leg is steered so it gives good control (but not as good as widely spaced twin props) and the leg is lifted to reduce drag when not in use. The disadvantages lie in getting the level right and the fact that it produces some noise. If set too high the prop can cavitate, thus losing drive, if set too low the prop will not be clear of the water when lifted.

Twin hydraulic drives from a single engine offers the attraction that the engine can be mounted anywhere (usually in the cockpit or nacelle) and the stern gear can be mounted in conventional stern tubes – for example, under aft cabin berths. The main disadvantages are a loss of power in the transmission and the weight and cost of the hydraulics.

A possible arrangement for some larger cats is to fit a standard single installation in one hull, and to use a small hydraulic power take-off from the front of the engine to drive a second prop in the other hull that is used solely for manoeuvring. The effect of the offset prop is minimal and does not affect straight-line steering. Along similar lines is the use of a saildrive coupled to a standard diesel generator as the manoeuvring second prop.

Propeller Drag and Folding Propellers

As the speed of a craft under sail increases, the effect of dragging a fixed-blade prop also increases. At 5 knots this drag could reduce speed by 0.25 knots, and at 10 knots the reduction could be 1 knot. As a result, there are numerous options for removing the props from the water, or folding or feathering when sailing.

Standard installations and saildrives obviously have to accept that the propellers stay in the water. The options for reducing drag here are between folding and feathering. The simplest folding propellers have hinged blades that spin open as the shaft turns and are folded down by the water flow when sailing. The disadvantage is some loss of efficiency in reverse. The Max Prop has flat blades that feather with the water flow and adopt the right angle of attack as the shaft rotates for forward or reverse. The Auto-Prop, priced between that of the Max Prop and the folding prop, is another patented blade system that feathers when the shaft is not rotating, but also adopts the optimum drive angle when the shaft is turning. There are a number of alternative controllable pitch props, but these are usually more expensive and only applicable in larger catamarans.

SUMMARY

- The wide base of the catamaran offers some advantages when supporting the mast and sheeting the sails. In all other ways the rig is similar to that on any other sailing yacht.

- Most catamarans come with a mainsail, a Genoa and a storm gib or staysail. For light winds the choice lies between the spinnaker and the cruising chute.

- Outboard motors, with solid-state electrics, offer a reliable, practical and economical answer to the question of auxiliary power. Twin outboards offer greater control.

5
PERFORMANCE AND HANDLING

For someone who has sailed a mono-hull the change to a catamaran is quite straightforward. He or she will quickly become familiar with the differences – primarily the effects of sailing upright, of more windage and of less weight.

Newcomers to sailing will find getting used to life aboard a catamaran and handling a catamaran much easier than the initiation on board a mono-hull. This is one reason why the catamaran makes such a suitable charter vessel – the charter customer quickly feels at home aboard the cat, while it may take a few days to gain the same familiarity aboard a mono-hull. If the charter is in the tropics the cat has the immediate advantage that the saloon is high, open plan and can be well ventilated.

Performance

Under Sail

As the catamaran is lighter in weight and has more stability than a mono-hull, its rig is both more efficient and more effective. Add to this the catamaran's slimmer hulls which are more easily driven through the water and do not have the same limiting factor as the wide beam mono-hull, and we have the potential for much improved performance. I say *potential* because not all cats are capable of sailing at high speed. Some of the advantage is partly offset by the greater windage of the cruising catamaran, and the actual performance will mostly depend on the water-line length and the sail area to weight ratio. The rather heavier cats with very conservative rigs will roughly match the performance of their mono equivalent, while the lighter types with tall sailplans will have substantially improved sailing performances. At the top end where performance is high on the designer's priority list, a spectacularly better speed will be achieved.

SAILING AT SPEED

When talking about sailing speeds it is most important to specify whether the figures given are top speeds which were achieved momentarily or average speeds that were maintained for a reasonable distance – or even those given by an inaccurate and over-optimistic log. Some wild claims are made for catamaran speeds, to the extent that the average speeds given in this section would appear to be totally at odds with the claims. Most of those speeds cannot be confirmed or have been achieved only in short bursts, perhaps helped along by wave action. To put the matter into true perspective, I like to look at the speeds achieved at the various speed trials that have been held over the years where accurate times are taken for a 500m (547yd) reaching course (where the highest speeds are achieved). The yachts taking part in past events have, for the most part, been out-and-out racers. It is most unlikely that a cruising cat could match these speeds, and hence claims for speeds in excess of the ones achieved at these events must be treated with some scepticism. On the measured 500m (547yd) stretch, it takes a very good 18m (60ft) boat to average 20 knots; 12m (40ft) catamaran is more likely to reach an average top speed of 16 or 18 knots. When a catamaran is sailing at high speed it is subject to constant accelerations and decelerations, so in order to achieve an average of 20 knots, the top speed could momentarily be as high as 25 knots. To average 15 knots over 1.6km (1 mile), the actual speed would vary by as much as 3 or 4 knots either way.

Under normal conditions, the highest speeds are clocked while surfing – something the catamaran does well and usually in complete safety. However, it is important to look out for the conditions which could lead to the odd steep wave causing excessive speed or broaching. It is not unusual for a quite average cruising catamaran, running with wind and waves, to ride a wave for a minute or two at speeds of 15 to 20 knots. As soon as the wave passes, its speed will drop back to 8 or 10 knots. Waves form, disperse and re-form so that it is not possible to ride one wave for any great distance.

A more practical figure for speed that will be of value to the cruising yachtsman is the average distance he is likely to cover in a typical passage. During a cruise on a loaded 9m (30ft) cruising catamaran, allow no more than 5 knots; if this was a 12–14m (40–45ft) boat with a good engine for use in light winds, it would be realistic to allow 7 knots as an average; at the same time, it is not unusual for a good 12m (40ft) cat to average 10 knots or more when conditions are favourable.

WINDWARD SAILING

As with any yacht, windward performance will depend a great deal on the style of craft. A high windage, moderate sail-plan cruising catamaran with low-aspect ratio keels will not be at its best with the wind on the nose. This is perfectly acceptable to a majority of cruising owners who plan their cruises to be enjoyable passages with the wind, rather than thrashing to windward all the way. Obviously, a reasonable windward performance can also be a safety factor should the yacht get into a situation when it needs to sail off a lee shore, so is not a subject that should be dismissed.

To get the best in windward performance, an efficient, sizeable sail area is needed, with good lateral resistance and low windage. The lighter weight catamaran needs the sail area to drive it through the waves, the most effective lateral resistance taking the form of deep keels or boards. The best windward results are achieved by keeping the catamaran moving at a good speed rather than attempting to sail too close to the wind. A good helmsman will tend to watch his speed log just as much as his close-hauled indicator when beating to windward. When sailing to windward, the catamaran does lack the feeling of sailing 'in the groove' that you get aboard a good-performance mono-hull – it is possible, in some circumstances, to stray from a close-hauled line on to a reach and not be aware of it until making a tack.

Most cruising catamarans are particularly good at motor-sailing to windward, perhaps with just one engine running. The engine keeps the speed up so that the craft powers through waves that might otherwise tend to stop the boat and reduce the drive from the sails.

When sailing a close-hauled course, the average cruising catamaran's performance is roughly equivalent to or even less than that of the cruising mono. Sometimes the same situation exists when sailing downwind in light wind. The cat's best speed is achieved in a good breeze when sailing on a reach.

COMPARING PERFORMANCE

There is a very simple formula that can be used for comparing sailing performance. This formula has become the basis for most rating rules used in racing. An example of when it can be applied is if a catamaran owner is considering re-rigging his yacht, perhaps to improve performance. What will be the increase in speed? By putting the figures into the following formula, the result gained will be the approximate boat speed (R) that will be achieved in a wind speed of 10 knots. The calculated change in speed with change in sail area will certainly be quite accurate.

$$R = 0.5 \sqrt{\frac{\text{LWL (in ft)} \times \text{sail area (in sq ft)}}{[\text{displacement (in lb)}]}}$$

When using this formula, it is worth working out the safety factors given in Chapter 6.

Under Power

An equally simple formula for calculating performance under power can also be used. Again, there are many other factors that are not taken into account so this cannot be expected to give precise figures. However, it will give a good indication for average conditions and will certainly give a good comparison between different boats or engine installations.

$$\text{Speed (in knots)} = \sqrt{\frac{\text{LWL (in m)} \times \text{engine output (in hp)}}{[\text{displacement (in tonnes)}]}}$$

Typical figures for an 11m (36ft) boat fitted with twin 18 horsepower diesels would look like this:

$$\text{Speed (in knots)} = \sqrt{\frac{10 \times 36}{[5]}} = 8.49$$

At higher than usual power to weight ratios, the speed given by the formula must be treated with more caution. My experience is that the formula is quite accurate for lightweight catamarans even for speeds up to 20 knots, but that it is over-optimistic for the heavier craft at higher speeds. For example, if twin 50 horsepower engines are fitted into the above 11m (36ft) cat, the figures become:

$$\text{Speed (in knots)} = \sqrt{\frac{10 \times 100}{[5]}} = 14.1$$

From experience, however, a top speed of about 12.5 or 13 knots would be expected.

From this formula you will see that the power is proportional to the square of the

Mannanan 76 – 20 knots under power.

speed. While it may be quite feasible to give a catamaran an engine producing a speed of 20 knots under power, due to the extra cost and extra weight most owners settle for a maximum speed in the 6 to 9 knot range.

There have been many attempts to produce the ultimate high-speed sailing yacht with high-speed performance under power. The cat does the job well, but it is the drag of the rig that limits the practicality of the concept.

Handling

When handling a catamaran, the first difference that will be noticed from a conventional yacht is that it is light and responsive – even to the wind when attempting to manoeuvre in harbour. As there is more windage and less of the boat in the water, a sudden gust will cause the boat to drift sideways quite rapidly. The use of twin propellers is no doubt the best option to keep control in such circumstances.

With the craft weighing less, it is usually easier to fend off from the quay or marina and this can be an asset on many occasions. Less weight combined with shallow draft also makes the business of running aground and drying out upright much less hazardous.

Sail Handling

Handling the sails of a catamaran is not much different from handling the sails of any other craft of the same size except for the fact that you are working from a more level platform. The only difficulty may occur when changing the headsail on the foredeck when sailing into the wind and waves. At such times the motion at the bow of a catamaran can be rapid enough to make it difficult to stay on your feet. However, today's, roller headsails, with control leads back to the cockpit, eliminate most of these tasks.

Recent years have seen the resurrection of roller boom systems. The mainsail (whether with full roach and full-length battens or normal roach) rolls into the boom on to a roller that is operated by a line which can be taken back to the cockpit. The alternative stowaway mainsail rolled into the mast is a more proven system and does reef and stow the sail with least effort. The disadvantage, however, is loss of roach area and added weight aloft in the mast section. With these systems the crew need never leave the cockpit to handle the mainsail and Genoa. The more usual mainsail is slab reefed. A section of the sail is pulled down to the boom by lines to a tack or a hook at the front of the boom and a line to the clew.

Halyards can either be left on the mast or brought back to the cockpit. Whether it is worth the extra blocks and lines to bring them back depends on the details of the system. My personal view is that it is not difficult to get to the mast and there is not a lot to be gained on a cat by having halyards in the cockpit.

On the larger cats, raising the fully battened mainsail can require quite a lot of

Halyards stowed at the mast.

effort. A good slide system is essential, particularly with full-length battens where the battens will otherwise tend to cause the slides to bind in the track. Stainless steel slides in an alloy track should be avoided. A two-part halyard may be fitted to the mainsail – a block is fitted to or into the head of the sail. When raised there is a lot of halyard tail to be stowed at the bottom of the mast, but it does mean that most of the hauling on the halyard can be done without using the winch. The arrangement also has the effect of reducing the compression in the mast due to the halyard tension. Making this change has been known to make the difference between having a mast section that is not quite strong enough and one that is perfectly adequate. The two-part halyard is also an asset when hauling someone to the masthead – the halyard load is easier to handle and hence safer, as well as requiring less effort.

Another option worth considering for cats over 12m (40ft) is to fit an electric winch. Sited on the top of the coachroof, it can be used for handling the halyards (via a turning block), the Genoa sheets and the anchor warp, if required.

The cat has a great advantage when it comes to the handling and sheeting of running sails. The wide working platform eliminates or reduces the need for poles to boom out sails. Without a pole a spinnaker is much more easily controlled while raising, setting and taking it down again. The asymmetric spinnaker, or cruising chute, offers even greater possibilities. It can be tacked on the centreline, to either side, or even to a pole on the centreline so that the tack is further forward. A well-equipped cruising catamaran will have a large spinnaker for downwind sailing in light winds and at least two cruising chutes – one for light winds and a smaller one that can be used in strong winds and close reaching. These running sails are sheeted from the deck edge. An alloy toe rail with snatch blocks is ideal for this purpose, but if there is no toe rail (many cats do not fit them) a number of 'U' bolts or convenient cleats will suffice for the average cruiser.

The size of the cockpit in the average catamaran presents the designer with a challenge. It sometimes happens that sail controls are arranged at each corner – port and starboard on the coachroof for the Genoa and port and starboard aft for the main traveller, the main sheet and the runners. Many attempts have been made to bring the controls together, with varying degrees of success. An arrangement that is particularly applicable on the larger and charter-size catamarans is the raised helm position where all the controls can be arranged around the position which is set into a permanent cockpit cover.

The mainsheet will normally run to a track and traveller. A convenient position for the main sheet winch is on the coachroof close to the helm. By taking the sheet forward to a block on the boom and down to another on the coachroof, the sheet does not have to be tended when tacking. The disadvantage of this system is that there is a loss of efficiency when the sheet is taken through the extra blocks. An alternative is the double-ended main sheet where the sheet runs from one end of the track, through the block system and to the other end of the track, where it will usually pass through a turning block to a winch beside the helm. The sheet runs through the blocks when tacking or when gybing. This has the effect of controlling the gybe to some extent.

Many mono-hulls have boom vangs fitted to hold the boom down when it is well outboard and the wind is aft. The wide main track and the ease of fitting preventers from the rail eliminate the need for a vang on a catamaran.

In the same way that the main track and traveller give full mainsail control over a wide angle, barber haulers can be set up to give similar control for the Genoa – a number of fixing points are needed. The use of twin Genoa tracks is another viable arrangement.

Most yachts are fitted with adequate auxiliary power, thus eliminating the need for some of the finer points of handling when under sail. However, it is worth trying these manoeuvres if only for the fun of it and to learn a little more about handling your boat. Working with the wide beam it is possible to manoeuvre a catamaran precisely using sails alone. This includes such manoeuvres as sailing backwards or backing out of marinas by backing the jib and main. A few cruising cats have wing masts that can be used in a similar way.

Anchoring

The first point to remember when planning to anchor is that a catamaran may become wind-rode due to the extra windage and the lower volume of hull in the water, while keel yachts are tide-rode. The latter can cause chaos as the tide turns, so give yourself plenty of room. The effect of windage can also cause the cat to

'sail' around the anchor, swinging first to one side and then to the other. The cure for this is to set the anchor to a bridle from each bow. The bridle can be fixed permanently to cleats on each bow with a loop into which the anchor warp can be tied. A simple bight of warp half-hitched into the loop in the bridle will be easy to undo.

Apart from these points, anchoring a catamaran is similar to anchoring any other vessel. Its reduced weight is offset by its greater windage and hence similar sized anchors are needed. To avoid the weight of a full-length anchor chain, it is usual for a catamaran to have a short length of chain with nylon warp making

An offset anchor roller.

Anchor bridle arrangement.

up the length. It is advisable to have a second anchor on any cruiser over about 9m (30ft) in length.

Handling a catamaran will almost certainly include at some stage going aground and attempting to get off again. It may mean using sails, engines or just a long pole from the deck. If these fail, a crewman in the water can be most effective.

SUMMARY

- Lighter in weight than the mono-hull and with more stability, the catamaran is both more effective and more efficient and has the potential for much improved performance, although not all catamarans are capable of sailing at high speed.

- The catamaran is more responsive to the wind than a conventional yacht. Twin propellers offer a means of control when attempting to manoeuvre in harbour.

- Sail handling on a catamaran is similar to that on any other craft of the same size. Modern systems allow most tasks to be carried out from the cockpit.

6
SAFETY

Overall safety covers every aspect of enjoying boating and minimizing the risk of damage to limb, life or craft. As with all pursuits, catamaran sailing is not entirely without risk – just being on the water adds to the risk. However, what risk there is can be reduced very considerably with knowledge, preparation and the right equipment.

Risks

Capsize

Capsize is the topic which has been associated with the catamaran throughout its modern development. It has been a particularly controversial subject in the past and it is for this reason that I deal with it first. In truth, however, capsize today is the least likely hazard the average catamaran owner is likely to encounter.

Contrary to what you may be lead to believe by some catamaran sales personnel, anything that floats can be capsized and catamarans are no exception, however unlikely that event may be. Every catamaran owner and skipper should have some idea of what the true risk is and what the situation is likely to be in such event. Without such facts he is unlikely to make the best decisions in such event.

The catamaran's stability is primarily a function of width, length and weight. A capsizing moment is the result of the effects of wind, waves and the momentum of sails, rigging, hull structure and so on. Obviously, a narrow, lightweight catamaran with a tall sailplan is much more likely to capsize than a heavy, wide beam catamaran. The other design factors that might contribute to a capsize are as follows:

1.   The likelihood of the cat tripping over a part of the hull that digs into a wave. This might be a bow, perhaps with little reserve buoyancy while surfing, or it might be a stern that digs in if the cat is thrown backward while beating into large waves.
2.   A tendency to pitch excessively. Very fine, narrow, double-ended hulls, perhaps with a tall rig, will pitch to a greater extent than usual. Such designs are more likely to suffer from digging in as outlined above.

Capsizes happen when too much sail is carried for the wind conditions, from wave action, from wave action in conjunction with the yacht's own momentum, a combination of the two, or all three together. It is obviously a complex subject. A detailed analysis is beyond the scope of this book and would be of little practical use to the owner or skipper anyway. Some of the few capsizes that do occur can be attributed to over-confidence or inexperience.

TOO MUCH SAIL

The simple capsize when there is too much sail in too much wind is easy to envisage. Some of the early production catamarans launched during the 1960s were narrow beam ones by today's standards, and a number did capsize in this way. Most were caught with too much sail up in a gust. Since the trend towards wider beam cats, there has been a big reduction in the numbers of capsizes in spite of the greatly increased numbers of cats afloat. To put the figures into context, during the ten-year period from 1980 to 1990 the Royal National Life-boat Institution (RNLI) were called out to just four large catamarans that had capsized in UK waters. Of these, only one was of British registration and at least one was an extreme racing cat. Obviously, the risk of capsize for the cautious owner sailing in home waters is of no great significance.

WAVE ACTION

It is easy to imagine a large, breaking wave picking up a catamaran and capsizing it in the process, but what actually happens in practice? Consider a 6m (20ft) wide catamaran lying a-hull, as it would if all the sails were dropped and the cat was left to its own devices. Any wave would obviously hit the windward hull first, so the theory has developed that the cat would come to little harm if allowed to slide sideways – in other words, if it does not have deep keels to prevent such sideways movement. The problem with this theory as the complete answer to the situation is that it all depends on the speed of the wave. Tank testing experiments have shown a wave hitting the windward hull, lifting it rapidly, but before too high an angle has been reached the wave has passed under the cat hitting the lee hull, and has brought the cat back on to an even keel. The truth is a combination of the two effects, with the latter perhaps being the most important factor. This does explain how some cats hit by breaking waves at other angles then beam-on have survived what the crew thought, if only momentarily, was a capsize situation. Most experienced cat sailors will remember occasions when beam-on waves have crashed against the hull with considerable impact. However, I do not know of any instances where damage has resulted to a modern, well built cat.

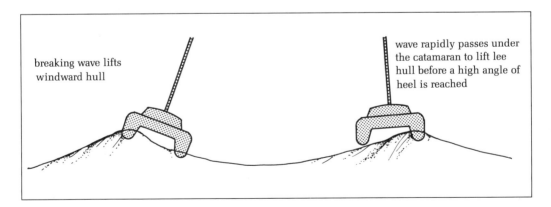

breaking wave lifts windward hull

wave rapidly passes under the catamaran to lift lee hull before a high angle of heel is reached

A catamaran on a breaking wave.

PRECAUTIONS FOR LONG-DISTANCE SAILORS

Long-distance sailing increases the chance of getting caught out in severe weather conditions. What precautions should the owner take? This is an area where there is little guidance to be found in builders' or designers' literature, and ideas do vary amongst experienced catamaran sailors. There are accounts of catamarans lying a-hull in storm conditions in perfect safety, other accounts report cats running with the wind and waves, and yet others have lain to sea anchors or streamed drogues.

I believe that the correct use of sea-anchors or drogues does substantially reduce the risk of capsize, but this is the one area of safety for which there is no realistic safety drill that can be put into practice before the event. Sailors who have used a sea-anchor or drogue in a storm will have had one particular system for that event and are very unlikely to get into a position to make any kind of comparative tests. It is therefore wise to only assess the theory and take note of the experience of the few who have put their particular system into practice.

It is my belief that there is no one single solution to storm conditions. A catamaran should carry some form of drogue to reduce surfing speeds, for conditions when there is plenty of sea room and the storm is taking you in the right direction. Other conditions could determine that lying to a sea-anchor could be the most suitable way of riding out a storm. Note the difference between these two devices – the drogue is a means of slowing the boat, while the sea-anchor should act very much as an anchor. Reports from those who have tried the latter suggest that setting a large sea-anchor from the bow has the immediate effect of calming the motion of the craft and producing a feeling of stability and security. A Tora 36 recently lay to a sea-anchor in the Gulf of Alaska for five days in winds up to 113kph (70mph). The sea-anchor must therefore be of sufficient size to act like an anchor and to stop any appreciable drift – if the device is too small the cat could drift backwards and is then likely to slew sideways, possibly increasing the likelihood of capsize.

The conditions of wind and waves will vary enormously and it is the combination of the two that the skipper has to assess. High winds alone should not present any danger to a well-reefed catamaran; regular high waves that are not breaking are equally unlikely to cause a problem. The worst situation is likely to arise with a wind change during a storm, perhaps combined with a strong current. I can offer no guidance for this situation, but hasten to remind you that the instances of cats surviving very severe storms are quite numerous. A number of racing multi-hulls have capsized in an area of the Atlantic just north of Bermuda. It is an area where the Gulf Stream meanders and I suspect that a confused sea in strong wind conditions could create a freak wave that is the likely cause of such capsizes. The solution is to try to avoid areas where such conditions are likely to exist.

WHAT HAPPENS WHEN YOU CAPSIZE?

What the situation is likely to be in the unlikely event of a capsize is of great importance. There have been cases of crews having a most uncomfortable time where a little knowledge could have improved the situation a lot. Any discussion of the subject starts by stating

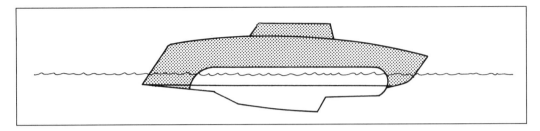

The usual position when capsized. The typical catamaran floats with the bridge-deck above the water-level, lying a-hull to the wind and waves.

that a catamaran does not sink like a ballasted mono-hull and makes a good raft. Although this is true it needs some further explanation.

Most cats are built of foam sandwich or timber and do have enough built-in buoyancy to ensure that they cannot sink. If, however, the cat is built of solid GRP and no effort is made to add buoyancy, it will sink if fully flooded. Normally, air would be trapped in the hulls but this may not be the case if one end goes down first.

Most capsized cats float with the bridge-deck just above the water-line, thus making a raft. At the same time, a flooded cat either way up has little stability and will be subject to a lot of motion due to wave action. Inside the average capsized cat, the hulls will be awash and waves will sweep from end to end. The effect is to wash out everything that is not fastened down, and, the inside is most inhospit-able, in anything other than a flat calm.

Very few standard cats will have any provision made for the capsize situation. Some builders may have added one or two sealed compartments, but that will be the extent of it. My suggestion when buying is that the potential owner should start by asking questions. The builder or the designer should be able to give you an idea of where the flotation level will be. This

will at least enable the owner to think about the problem and to plan his course of action in the unlikely event.

The crew can gather on the bridge-deck, but they will need something to hang on to. A shelter could be built, but this needs attachment points. If you have a life-raft, the inflated raft attached securely on the bridge-deck would be my first choice, followed by a dinghy lashed to the bridge-deck. Ask yourself how difficult it will be to get to the raft – ideally it will be accessible from the upturned craft and lashed on to the bridge-deck with a few 'U' bolts.

A useful and very simple arrangement for crew to hang on to in the event of a capsize is a length of strong line that runs under the bridge-deck, fore and aft and firmly attached at both ends. It also has other uses: if you wish to inspect the bridge-deck from the dinghy, the line is used to pull the dinghy through; or swimmers can use the line in a similar fashion. Another simple recommendation is that the underside of the bridge-deck should be painted orange or yellow so that it stands out in a breaking sea where the usual white structure would look like just another breaking wave.

The likely conditions within a capsized hull should be understood. As mentioned above, there will be waves inside the hulls, washing from end to end unless there are doors that can be closed. Unless there is a planned survival compartment, survival suits or good foul-weather gear are likely to provide better shelter on the bridge-deck than inside the hulls of the average cat.

GUSTS

What do you do in the event of a gust that could threaten capsize? The instinctive reaction is to luff. There is a good chance that there will be a change of wind direction with the gust, and hence my advice is to luff if close-hauled, but if reaching or if you are in any doubt, the best action is to turn away from the wind rapidly until it is on the quarter. The boat speed will reduce the apparent wind speed and hence the pressure on the sails. Obviously, the sails will need adjusting and attention to steering will be important until the sails are set correctly.

The whole question of catamaran capsize has been a controversial one for many years, fuelled by a few capsizes amongst racing craft and by the prejudice of some traditional sailors. In reality, the record for cruising catamarans paints a very different picture.

Fire

It is often argued that because a cat does not sink it makes a good raft. The crew should always stay with the boat and hence a cat need not carry a dedicated life-raft. I subscribe to this view, provided that there is an adequate tender (probably a reasonable sized inflatable equipped with survival gear) to cater for the consequences of a fire aboard the cat. Most cats

will be constructed of GRP, and once a fire takes hold it will burn fiercely and quickly. Being prepared for such an event is the best answer. Precautions such as the use of gas detectors, painting the galley with intumescent paints or resins and keeping inflammables in a separate self-draining compartment are to be recommended, and will reduce the risk of fire to a very low and acceptable level. The self-draining compartment is particularly easy to arrange in a cat because there are compartments that can be drained through the bridge-deck, without having to drain into the bilge.

Running Aground

Running aground in a cat is usually no-where near as hazardous as it can be with a deep-ballast keel. The cat is much easier to get off, the water will be shallower and the boat remains upright. If you are unlucky enough to get caught on a lee shore, the cat again usually has the advantage. There have been cases of cats riding up over reefs and of others being carried up on to rocks or a beach, remaining upright throughout, and with the crew stepping off safely and unharmed. In some instances the cat has even been floated off later with little damage done. The deep-keel yacht in a similar situation will hit the rocks or beach in much deeper water, will be at risk of rolling over and its extra weight will prevent the waves from washing it into shallow water.

Collision with Another Vessel

Accidents due to collision are no more or less likely to happen to a cat than any other vessel on the sea. A good lookout and experience are the best insurance. The fact that the cat is less likely to sink, however, is a plus in the collision situation.

Personal Injury or Falling Overboard

Again, this is a hazard on any craft. However, the fact that the cat sails upright means that getting around is a lot easier and the cat should therefore be less prone to such accidents.

The problem of getting back aboard a catamaran after accidentally falling overboard should be considered. Most cats now have steps in the transom, and a swim ladder that folds down into the water is all that is needed for an able-bodied member of crew. Getting an injured crew member back on board is likely to be a different matter, and the safety procedures in the event of such a situation should be practised regularly.

Lightning

Lightning is not a hazard that sailors are particularly concerned with in the UK. In parts of the world such as the east coast of the USA, however, there is considerable concern with regards to lightning. Providing a path for the lightning strike so that it takes the line of least resistance to the water is the usual method of prevention – a heavy cable from the masthead that leads to a conductor in the water can be routed on a cat without going through a hull, thereby eliminating the risk of blowing a hole in the hull.

Collision with Floating Debris

Our seas and oceans are littered with

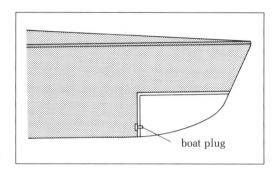

The crash box is built into each bow.

floating debris, but this is not always visible and cannot be seen at night. To prevent damage from such debris, it is a relatively simple matter to build in a crash box at the most vulnerable area of each bow. In its simplest form, the crash box is a built-in tank with a boat drain fitted at the lowest point aft so that it can be checked for water ingress and can be drained. In the event of flooding from another source it provides added flotation, so the larger it is the better. There is often an area aft in each hull, perhaps under a bunk, that is difficult to get at for stowage purposes – such an area can also be turned into a crash box. Sailors should also note that there is a theory that the current trend towards plumb stem cats increases the risk of damage because the boat is less likely to ride up over the debris.

Breaking Up

Prompted by tales of racing cats breaking up, this is a topic that is often raised. It is very rare indeed for the bridge-deck saloon catamaran to suffer damage to its cross structure. The bulkheads and the decking form a very deep structural beam, and unless they are very poorly designed or built, such structures will very easily cope with the stresses imposed by all normal sailing conditions. Without the need to achieve the ultimate in light weight for racing, even the open bridge-deck types should never be at risk.

Damage at the connection between the bridge-deck and the hull is a slightly more common occurrence. The cause is usually a combination of too little bridge-deck clearance, overloading and poor design or assembly. The problem arises more with plywood-built cats where the join is more difficult to engineer than with GRP-production catamarans.

Safety Equipment and Features

Parachute Sea-Anchors

Parachute sea-anchors come in a variety of types. The least expensive type can be bought from an army surplus store, is usually about 6m (20ft) in diameter and was originally made for dropping cargo from aircraft. A long length of suitable nylon warp will be required, with swivels, a means of securing it to the catamaran and a means of tripping when the storm is over. A sea-anchor is one that will hold the vessel virtually anchored to the sea. I have

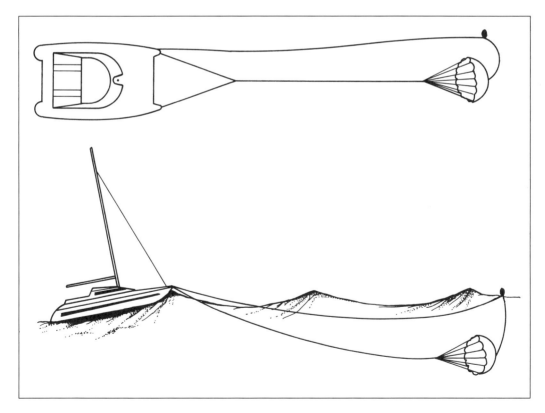

The sea-anchor.

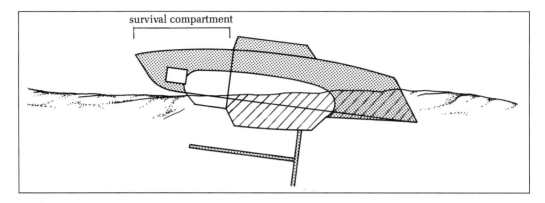

survival compartment

The survival compartment. It needs a strong door, a bilge pump and an escape hatch (or means to cut through the hull).

a report of a sea-anchor towing a 16m (52ft) catamaran with the current against a storm off the east coast of South Africa.

It seems that the diameter of a sea-anchor should be close to the beam of the catamaran. The length of the nylon line needs to be between 100m (328ft) and 150m (492m) and equal to the anchor line in diameter. A tripping line is required to retrieve the sea-anchor. Retrieval is another instance where the catamaran has an advantage over the mono-hull – as the breaking wave hits from the bow, the finer hulls of the cat cut through the wave, creating less impact and meaning that the bow will not be thrown as high out of the water.

Drogues

A drogue is a device used to produce drag – as the speed of being towed through the water increases the resistance increases by the square of the speed. Hence, they are capable of producing a considerable force at the right time. A drogue is usually used to slow the boat in high winds or to stop it gaining too much speed while surfing. It can consist of any device which is trailed in the water – for example, weighted tyres, the regular anchor itself or specially made items.

Survival Compartments

Capsize survival compartments have been proposed for catamarans but few have actually been built. Not a great deal is needed in terms of equipment and the compartment could add enormously to the crew's comfort. A good, reasonably water-tight door, a pump and a means of ventilation, escape and lookout are the essentials – an aft cabin is probably the best location for such a compartment. The watertight door will stop the water sweeping into the compartment, and keeping pace with leaks around a reasonable door should not be too great a task for the pump. In my view, this is well worth the small investment for those who intend to sail across oceans. The first positive effect is to add buoyancy to that corner of the cat – this will lift the area so that an escape hatch is more effective, and will also add stability to the 'raft'.

An escape hatch at hull side.

Escape Hatches

Some races and some regulations (*see* Safety Regulations in France on page 84) require the fitting of escape hatches to catamarans, and a number of production catamaran builders fit escape hatches as standard. They are usually fitted into the inboard hull side, between the water and bridge-deck, and are usually outward opening deck hatches. Most have been entirely satisfactory, but such a feature must be strong to resist wave and debris impact. A secondary means of closing off the opening – such as a panel fixed on the inside – is worth consideration. Ideally, there will be an escape hatch in each hull.

For an escape hatch to be most effective, it needs to be above the water-line when the cat is in a capsized position. Buoyancy built into the deck-head as extra insulation is worth considering for this purpose. The escape hatch should not be in the bridge-deck itself, as if in that position it would be difficult to get through because it will be close to the water. The hatch must be recessed in such a way that the water flow does not impact on the hatch seal.

Other uses for the escape hatch can be for providing ventilation when there is no fear of waves washing in, using it for viewing under the bridge-deck, and even for changing a prop for a sonic leg.

Staying With the Boat

Experience tells us that in the event of a capsize or accident it is better to stay with the boat if at all possible. There may be a time in such a situation that getting into a life-raft could seem an attractive proposition, however, the advice is to do so as a last resort only. In spite of its name, a life-raft is a small, flimsy affair with very little room and few comforts. Surviving in one for any length of time is a traumatic experience.

In view of the fact that catamarans do not sink, many cat owners dispense with the life-raft altogether and instead equip their dinghy to be used as a life-raft in the event of fire, which is the only time that you should leave the yacht itself.

Masthead Buoyancy

A few narrow beam catamarans are still sailing with a masthead float as a legacy of the 1960s. The theory at the time was that the cat would lie on its side rather than turn a full 180 degrees. However, none of the modern designs use them as it is believed that the weight and windage of the masthead buoyancy could be the last straw that ensures the cat does capsize when it might otherwise come back to the vertical.

Self-Righting Systems

A number of self-righting systems have been proposed over the years and some have been tested, but none has as yet been developed sufficiently to be sold as a fully-tested system. In theory, the problem is not difficult, with most systems involving partial flooding and applying a righting moment. Controlled flooding reduces stability and the righting moment required does not need to be great – the weight of a full water bag on the end of a lever arm is the usual suggestion, but air bags are probably a more viable alternative.

The first problem with developing such a system is that any testing of it is unlikely to be entirely satisfactory until it is carried out in real-life capsized conditions, and by that time it will be too late if anything has been overlooked. Amongst catamaran owners, the interest in such systems is minimal. For the average cruising cat, in my view, the risk of capsize is so low that it is valid to give full consideration to survival compartment(s) and the sea-anchor precautions, and to leave the self-righting ideas for those who might be contemplating rounding Cape Horn or similar.

Stability Number

There has recently been a proposal that every catamaran should have a stability number displayed within the craft. Nothing has been finalized by the time of writing, but a guide to the idea is given below – the responsibility, however, must rest with the skipper on board at all times. An experienced sailor, who is totally familiar with his craft, may not have any use for the information, but it will be of help to the less experienced, whether they be a skipper or helmsman.

The stability formula given below shows the wind speed at which the windward hull will (in simplest theory) lift, and is generally accepted within the industry. It is certainly not a precise figure and obviously numerous other factors which are not taken into consideration here will affect the behaviour of a catamaran at sea. These factors are: true direction of the resultant sail force, wind angle to the boat, angle of heel, the cut of the sails, the sheeting of the sails, the sea state, the windage of the hull and rig, the configuration of keels and rudders, waterline length and so on. A total analysis of all the possible configurations would be a most complex issue.

Wind speed at which hull will lift =

$$K \times \sqrt{\frac{Wt \times CL \text{ of boat to CL of lee hull} \times k}{[SA \times Ht \text{ of CoA}]}}$$

Wt = displacement of boat, CL = centreline, SA = sail area, Ht of CoE = height of centre of effort above waterline.

For wind speed: in knots, K = 13.7; in mph, K = 15.8; in kph, K = 25.4.
Using imperial units: Wt is in lb; distance is in ft; SA is in sq ft; k = 1.
Using metric units: Wt is in kg; distance is in m; SA is in sq m; k = 0.2.

To make use of this figure, we need to allow a margin for gusts. As a general rule I suggest 30 per cent as a reasonable figure. However, there are times, such as in thunderstorm conditions, when the gusts can be very much higher. Such conditions do not usually last for any great length of time and the skipper should be able to interpret the situation accordingly.

An example using the figures for the Suncat 36:

Length at water-line (LWL) = 10m, Wt = 3.9 tonnes, SA = 60.2 sq m, Ht of CoE = 6.8m, CL of boat to CL of lee hull = 2.1m.

Wind speed at which hull will lift

$$\text{(in knots)} = 13.7 \times \sqrt{\frac{3,900 \times 2.1 \times 0.2}{[60.2 \times 6.8]}}$$

$$[= 27.4 \text{ knots}]$$

Allowing a 30 per cent margin for gusts = 27.4 ÷ 1.3 = 21 knots.

Another example using figures for the Suncat 40:

LWL = 11.07, Wt = 4,550kg, SA = 81.6 sq m, Ht of CoE = 7.8m, CL of boat to CL of lee hull = 2.7m.

Wind speed at which hull will lift

$$\text{(in knots)} = 13.7 \times \sqrt{\frac{4,550 \times 2.7 \times 0.2}{[81.6 \times 7.8]}}$$

$$[= 26.9 \text{ knots}]$$

Allowing a 30 per cent margin for gusts = 26.9 ÷ 1.3 = 20.7 knots.

Perhaps the most important factor when assessing the significance of this wind speed is the direction of sailing relative to the wind. In other words, do we treat this wind speed as true wind or apparent wind? The reaching, apparent wind can be equivalent to true wind plus 25 per cent, so it is not an insignificant difference. However, it can be argued that in the reaching situation the increase in apparent wind is due to the boat speed, which is due to the wind component driving the boat forward. Hence, it is practical to use the true wind as the capsizing force in the formula above.

A problem is more likely to arise when sailing off the wind – the wind instruments will show a reading less than the true wind. Rounding up could produce an even bigger difference between the apparent and true wind speed and some surprises for the unwary. There is obviously no simple rule to follow, but it is important to be aware of the stability number and having a figure as a starting-point must be well worth while.

If I was sailing with an inexperienced helmsman I would ask him to call me at any time that the wind speed instrument indicated a reading over the margin figure, and to warn him of the false sense of security when sailing downwind. Both Suncat examples given above are moderate beam cats with high sailplans and the weight figures are in the lightly loaded condition. Heavier cats with shorter sailplans will give higher figures for the wind speed at which the hull will lift.

Obviously, the factors not allowed for in the formula are significant and we know from experience that the above figures are rather pessimistic. I maintain that the figures are a good guide for the beginner and should be followed until sufficient experience has been gained in a variety of different conditions. For example, in strong winds as soon as a reef is taken in, the height of the centre of effort is lowered dramatically, the boat will feel a lot more comfortable and there will usually be little or no loss of speed.

Safety Regulations in France

The French authorities have much stricter rules for off-shore sailing than the rest of the world. To be able to take a French yacht off-shore unrestricted, it must have a Class 1 certificate. To get this certificate a catamaran has to have (amongst other requirements) a certain amount of flotation built in, and it must also have an escape hatch (500mm, 19.7in, diameter) on each side.

There are likely to be new regulations coming to all countries within the Common Market, but these are still to be decided.

SUMMARY

- Minimize what risks there are with knowledge, preparation and the right equipment.

- Capsize occurs as a result of carrying too much sail for the wind conditions, from wave action, from wave action in conjunction with the yacht's own momentum, a combination of two, or from all three acting at once.

- In the event of capsize always stay with the boat. Only in the event of fire should a life-raft or inflatable be used.

- The correct use of sea-anchors or drogues reduces the risk of capsize.

7

FAMILY CRUISING AND LONG-DISTANCE SAILING

Many yachts are advertised in a tropic island setting. Such a setting is the dream of many yacht owners, and this dream is becoming a reality for increasing numbers.

Family Cruising

The catamaran is particularly suitable where comfort and family sailing or permanent living aboard is the main purpose of the yacht. There are several reasons for this, in particular, the extra comforts that the catamaran provides.

Space and Privacy

When sailing a single-hull yacht the crew are thrown together with little room for privacy, and even the saloon often has to double as a sleeping cabin for some of the crew. Many a major cruise has been planned, only to fall apart on the first leg of the journey simply because of friction between members of crews who are living closely together for perhaps the first time. The catamaran not only has more space, but its layout allows separate private cabins, often with their own private toilets. The usual catamaran layout consists of a cabin in each end of each hull, with a central saloon and galley. Each crew member can therefore retire to his or her own cabin.

Headroom

Most cruising cats which are over about 7.6–8.5m (25–28ft) in length have standing headroom in the hulls and sitting headroom in the saloon. Those over about 10.6m (35ft) usually have good standing headroom in the saloon as well. The in-hull headroom is achieved in one of two ways: by extending the coachroof sufficiently far over the hull, (this can, however, leave very narrow side-decks) or by raising the side-decks to give headroom underneath.

Insulation and Ventilation

These are two features that are particularly important and can be well arranged in a catamaran. Insulation is built in where foam is used in the construction – if it is not, then I strongly recommend that you add it to your boat if you intend to spend any length of time aboard. Insulation will reduce condensation and provide a more comfortable environment whether it is cold or hot.

Where bunks are set on to the bridge-deck, it is important to have space between the mattress and the bridge-deck. If not, condensation will have you looking for phantom leaks.

The deck of the catamaran is well above sea level and is rarely subject to waves reaching that level. Hence, arranging ventilation is simpler than doing so to the equivalent mono-hull. Opening deck hatches are usual and there is plenty of deck area for them on the cat. In the tropics an open deck hatch fitted with a wind

scoop can turn a stiflingly hot cabin into a cool sleeping berth.

Bunk Fittings

Many catamaran bunks are fitted in the hulls. At first the width may seem restricted, but as crew members can roll against the hull side there is usually plenty of room. Many cat designs use either a flared hull or a step in the hull and bridge-deck to give extra width. The flare is perhaps the more elegant solution, but the step can be equally effective and has other uses – for example, it can be used as the first step down into the hull from the bridge-deck or even to provide an area of full standing headroom at a chart table. It

A cockpit cover on the Sunrise.

A cockpit cover on the Sunbeam.

also has the effect of adding stiffness and reducing the bridge-deck panel size.

Cockpit Covers

The usual bridge-deck catamaran has a natural cockpit protection in the saloon bulkhead at the front of the cockpit. To date, the majority of cat designs have not gone further and followed the mono-hull norm where the crew and anyone in the cockpit is unprotected from the elements. Why should the helmsman have to don his foul-weather gear every time? This need not be the case, and more cats are designed now with protection for the cockpit from water, wind and sun. Protection from the sun, for many, is just as important as from wind or rain.

Making the cockpit into the main living area is an attraction for some cat owners. The cat layout lends itself to the design of this feature in such a way that it can be used while sailing. Many combinations are possible, from folding screens and bimini-style tops, to solid tops and so on. Obviously, a simple boom tent for use in harbour is easily arranged. On the larger cats, particularly those aimed at charter hire, there are designs that include a raised helm position, through a solid cover over all or part of the cockpit. This has the added advantage that it is an easy matter to bring all the sail controls to one

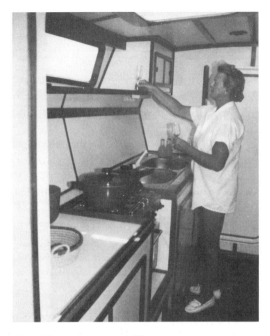

The galley in a 14m (45ft) boat.

area and away from other crew members in the cockpit who are not directly involved in sailing the yacht.

The Galley

The galley aboard a catamaran, where it is positioned in one hull, is usually closer to the size you would expect in a house kitchen than the usual space allotted on most mono-hull yachts. Some designs offer the galley on the bridge-deck as this has the advantage that the cook is not cut off from the rest of the crew – obviously, however, this does restrict the size of the galley.

Toilets and Showers

Thanks to upright sailing, toilets and showers can be used without too much

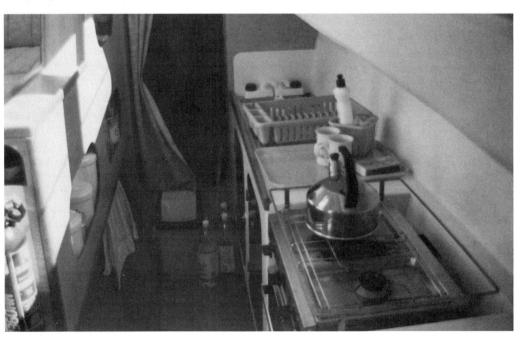

The galley in a 7.3m (24ft) boat.

discomfort while under way, and most cats over 10.6m (35ft) have more than one toilet. The only problem comes when sailing to windward in waves if the toilet is right up forward. It is worth while having at least one toilet positioned well aft in the boat.

Holding Tanks

To comply with the regulations of various countries, it is worth while having at least one toilet arranged to pump to a holding tank. If only for occasional use, this can be in the crash area which is built in at each bow.

Children

Whether toddlers or teenagers, children readily take to sailing aboard a cat. Something can usually be found to keep them amused – from play pools in the cockpit, a Jaccuzi on the foredeck, and from games in the saloon without the feeling of being confined, to a quiet afternoon in their own private cabin. As soon as they become big enough to see over the wheel or strong enough to handle a winch, children also become useful members of the crew.

Long-Distance Sailing

Long-distance cruising involves spending a lot of time on board, carrying all your stores for a period of weeks, and not always being able to run for shelter if the weather forecast is unfavourable. Choosing the best boat for the job is essential and will almost certainly make the difference as to whether the cruise is a success for everyone on board or not.

Those factors listed in Chapter 6 must be of paramount importance, but if everyone is going to enjoy the experience, comfort and practicality will also be major factors. Most long-distance cruises are undertaken at the most favourable time of the year and may involve trade-wind sailing. Chapter 3 lists the features that need to be considered. There is no doubt that the right catamaran will fill the requirements very adequately, and for most it will be the best choice. Caution must be placed on this careful choice, however, particularly with reference to size and carrying capacity.

You might think that shallow draft would not be an important consideration for long-distance cruising, but this is far from the case. I remember talking to a couple who had spent seven years cruising around the world in a superbly luxurious 17.3m (57ft) deep-keel yacht with 2m (6½ft) draft. Their ambition was to go back in a catamaran and visit the many places, particularly the harbours on islands in the Pacific Ocean, that they had to sail past because of the restriction imposed by their draft. With a draft of 1m (3ft) or less, vast areas open up for exploration – for example, much of southern Florida and the Bahamas have thousands of miles of water 1–2m (3–6ft) deep and not much tide. The catamaran can go almost anywhere, but the conventional yacht must keep to the deep channels. When you arrive at that tropic island anchorage you will first see the mono-hulls anchored in the deep water. You will be able to pass between them and anchor in the shallower water or even close to the beach – you might even decide to tie up to a palm tree. The mono-hulls' crews will have a long row in their dinghy, while the members of your crew can simply take off their shoes and wade ashore.

FAMILY CRUISING AND LONG-DISTANCE SAILING

I like to compare sailing to flying. The middle of a wide ocean is equivalent to being at an altitude of several thousand feet in an aircraft – there is not a lot of variety in scenery to hold your interest and there is little sensation of speed. On the other hand, sailing in shallow water is like flying close to the ground, but in a cat it is without danger. Beaching in shallow water can just be a way of getting ashore, or can be for a quick repaint or repair. The cruiser's dream situation – tied up to a palm tree on a warm sandy shore – is more realistic when you are in a catamaran.

The reasons a yachtsman or woman crosses oceans are multitudinous. The satisfaction may be of achieving a long-term ambition, being master of your own small world, seeing new places, or getting away from it all. The first time I sailed across the Atlantic in the early 1960s we set off with a log, a reasonably accurate watch, a radio receiver, a sextant, navigation tables and a few charts. The radio receiver was our only contact with the rest of the world, and the greatest satisfaction came when the expected headland appeared at the time and place anticipated after a period of weeks without sight of land. Today's navigational aids and low-cost radio equipment have changed the whole nature of ocean-crossing in small yachts, and older navigators may regret this progress that has taken away the challenge of navigation. For example, a simple and inexpensive satellite navigation instrument gives you your latitude and longitude by pressing a few buttons. There is still usually plenty to do aboard a yacht, however, and obviously there is still the same tremendous sense of achievement. There is the challenge of being your own master on board your own vessel, and in charge of your own destiny.

I count myself lucky in that my first passage was on a trimaran, and this has lead to a life-long interest in the varied world of boats. On my first trade-wind crossing of the Atlantic in 1963 I was on board a 10m (33ft) trimaran in the Canary Islands for two months during the high season for the crossing. This was the time that the trimaran was just beginning to make its mark as a world cruising yacht type. We met up with another four or five trimarans and just one cat on the same route. That represented a substantial proportion of the total transatlantic fleet of about twenty-five such craft, but today I imagine that the proportion would be the other way round with at least five cats to every trimaran on the route. In 1963 the proportion was representative of the feelings at the time – the typical cat had a fairly narrow beam and was not generally considered to be suitable for serious off-shore work. The wider beam trimarans were generally considered to be more capable of coping with the seas.

Both catamarans and trimarans have increased their beams over the years. Designers have learned that there is much to be gained and nothing to be lost with a wider beam – at least, up to a point. In my view, over-extreme beam loses the point as the effective size, cost and motion at sea are all more a function of length multiplied by breadth than of length alone. For example, taking a 10m (33ft) cruising cat which is 5.5m (18ft) wide, the beam could be increased to 7.3m (24ft) on the same length and the cat would still work, or both could be increased to give the same length to beam ratio, resulting in a 12 × 6.4m (40 × 21ft) craft. The latter would certainly achieve better overall average speed, and would have equal or better diagonal stability plus a better

The saloon in a Kelly 45.

motion at sea. The extreme beam would have better athwartship stability, but this ignores other factors such as overall stability.

If cost restrictions are ignored, the ideal size of catamaran to choose for a major voyage for the average family would probably be 12–15m (40–50ft) long. A boat over 12m (40ft) long with, say, a 6.7m (22ft) beam is classified as big. At realistic budgets, however, most families will be looking at cats in the 9.8–13.7m (32–45ft) range.

My personal preference for long-distance sailing would be a cat in the wide-beam style, with minimum fixed draft and I would definitely be carrying a sea-anchor on board. I would also carry a good sized inflatable dinghy equipped to carry out the role of life-raft.

Most long-distance cruises are via trade-wind routes – in other words, going with the wind and the waves. In conditions such as these where a mono-hull is perhaps at its least comfortable, the catamaran quite simply excels.

SUMMARY

- For family cruising and long-distance sailing, the catamaran offers many plus points including space and privacy, sufficient headroom, good insulation and ventilation, cockpit cover and an ample galley size.

- The catamaran is an ideal craft for exploring away from deep channels.

- For the average family, a 12–15m (40–50ft) catamaran would be the ideal for a major voyage. Budgetary restrictions may mean a 9.7–13.7m (32–45ft) size is chosen.

- Carry a sea-anchor and a good sized inflatable dinghy to act as life-raft.

8
CATAMARAN RACING

The Dinghy Catamaran

The dinghy sailing catamaran (or beach cat) has well-established classes and regular races in most parts of the UK. The Hobie Cat, Dart Catamaran and Prindle Catamaran are typical, with international competitions catering to these types. The attraction of racing these catamarans is fast and exciting sailing. Some are narrow enough to be trailed or they are demountable for trailing, and the smaller dinghy catamarans can even be carried on top of a car for ease of transportation. Although raced with one or two crew, these cats can carry more when fun sailing.

An owner-built Tonga 39 in the West Indies.

A micro racer Leo 25 on its trailer.

The Cruising or Racing Catamaran

When racing sailors graduate to a larger family cruiser, many would like to continue in racing without having to own two boats. Unfortunately, there are not as many events open to the cruising catamarans as we would like to see. A significant proportion of cruising yacht owners take part in local club races and events such as the Round the Island Race (Isle of Wight). Today, clubs which organize races often include a separate multi-hull class, or attempt to rate them and include them in their current race programme. The number of multi-hulls taking part in such events, however, is usually quite small – contact your local yacht club to find out what the situation is in your area.

Many newcomers to sailing find that the interest in getting the best performance from their yachts develops as their confidence and skills increase. Sailing in close quarters with other yachts is the best way to judge your own sailing skills and the performance of your craft. You only have to spend a short time in the club bar to realize the pride most owners take in the performance of their craft – and the yachts do not have to be the latest in racing style. Multi-hull owners are no different in this respect.

A Typhoon trimaran.

In spite of the success of the multi-hull as a racing machine, attempts to provide the cruising catamaran owner with a regular racing programme have met with less success. The Crystal Trophy, from Cowes to Plymouth via Bishop Rock, organized by the British Multihull Offshore Cruising and Racing Association (MOCRA), was a popular event that started in 1967. It was the main event for the cruising and fast-cruising cat owner for a number of years, and attracted a fleet of fifteen to twenty multi-hulls of various sizes for each event. Unfortunately, with the appearance of faster racing craft, the numbers dwindled and the event was dropped from the calendar. Attempts to organize similar events since have met with limited success. Today, the Round the Island Race is the major event. It has a good multi-hull entry and is well worth the effort of getting to the start line.

In the major long-distance races such as the Round Britain Race and Transatlantic Races organized by the RWYC, a small number of entries have been fast cruising catamarans as opposed to extreme racing machines, and these have put up very creditable performances. These cats tend to be one-off designs, but they do illustrate

A Strider.

The Micro Multihull Class

The Micro Multihull Class is quite a popular racing class, with fleets in a number of countries and various races held throughout the season. These 8m (26ft) trailerable cats and tris have a minimum of three berths, and make reasonable cruisers for a young crew which also wants to take part in a few races. Most are perfectly seaworthy and the races are competitive, but if you want comfort this is not the class for you.

Other races that deserve a mention are the AZAB (Azores and Back) and the Three Peaks Races. The AZAB offers the choice of single-handed or two-handed, and separate classes for multi-hulls. The Three Peaks Races are a test of sailing skills, combined with running up and down mountains for two of the crew. The multi-hull comes into its own both for its sailing performance, for its shallow draft and for its low weight. Rowing is allowed, and the combination of all these factors gives the advantage to the cats and tris which are usually invincible.

Major Open Races

To have any chance of winning a major open race, a custom-designed and built multi-hull racing machine is essential. As a result, most of those taking part in current events are sponsored. With the publicity and popularity of such events, no cruising catamaran would stand a chance. To give an idea of the achievement of such a craft, the current record for crossing the Atlantic from west to east is held at an average of 18 knots. Such craft are extremely interesting, but lie beyond the scope of this book.

a concept that offers truly exciting performance combined with reasonable accommodation. A typical such catamaran would be 15.2m (50ft) in length, with an 8.2m (27ft) beam, and a simple interior and equipment. Kept simple, such a cat will cruise at 6 or 7 tonnes of displacement. A good size sailplan will give sailing speeds in the low teens (knots) with little effort. The more common cruising-style catamaran with all the usual gear will be 5 tonnes or more heavier. As a one-off, however, fast cruising cats are not the most economical to have built or to campaign, but they will certainly give the maximum enjoyment while making fast passages under sail.

A Firebird.

Inside the Strider.

Races Along the UK's South Coast

As mentioned above, the racing scene for catamarans is not as successful as it might be. However, during the summer an enthusiast with the right catamaran could race every weekend at organized races on the south coast of England. Relatively small numbers take part, and the events do need better promotion if they are to attract more catamaran owners and more organization from catamaran sailors. This situation is certain to improve as more cats take to the water.

Future Races

A hope I have for the future is that races will be arranged to fill the gap between the extreme custom-built machines and the relatively heavy catamaran cruisers that are the majority today. With the increasing popularity of the cat, it should be possible to renew interest in racing good performance cats that are also suitable for cruising. Such races could be a one-design class or, more likely, they would be run on somewhat similar lines to the Micro Multihull Class but with rules that cater to a greater extent for cruising requirements.

There is no doubt that design progress made for racing does filter down to other types of catamarans. Currently, however, the top racing machines are so far removed that this potential has been lost to the cruiser. The performance of the new racer/cruiser I envisage would be well above the average performance that we see in most cats today. The structure could be built from a lightweight sandwich at a reasonable cost and, provided the rules are written to exclude excessively tall sailplans, the results would be attractive vessels that sail fast yet still fulfil their role as family cruisers.

Rating Rules

Various rating rules have been devised to assess the potential performance of craft wishing to race. Such rules for mono-hulls have met with limited success, and have lead to a lot of controversy and a lot of work for designers who search for loopholes in the measurement rules. The catamaran has an advantage in this respect. It can be weighed relatively simply, and this sidesteps the problems that have been associated with mono-hull rules. The weight will then give a measure of both the stability and resistance of the craft – a simple rule can therefore be applied to a fleet of cruiser/racer cats and be expected to produce acceptable results most of the time.

SUMMARY

- Local yacht clubs will be able to furnish details of events for multi-hulls.

- For the major races, a custom-built craft is essential.

- The Multihull Offshore Cruising and Racing Association (MOCRA) can be contacted via Janice Uttley, 1 Ward Crescent, Emsworth, Hampshire, PO10 7RR, UK.

9

PRODUCTION CATAMARANS AND CUSTOM DESIGNS

For many years the UK was the major catamaran producer, filling the home market and exporting to Europe and the US. Prouts and Catalac were responsible for getting the largest numbers on to the water. During the past seven or eight years, however, French producers, with considerable encouragement from the French government, have taken the lead with companies such as Fountain Pajot, Jeantot, Kennex and Catana in the fore. Catamaran builders are usually specialists and it is rare for established mono-hull builders to take on catamaran production. Jeanneau is one exception, and offers three models at 12.8m (42ft), 14.3m (47ft) and 16.8m (55ft). In both the UK and France there are numerous catamaran builders who produce in smaller numbers – both production and one-off custom craft.

All the production builders work in glass-reinforced polyester (GRP) from production moulds. Interior moulds are also used in many cases. Due to the relatively large areas of flat surface on a catamaran and the advantage of light weight, the use of some form of sandwich construction is also usual, giving strength and stiffness for minimum weight. The sandwich consists of a PVC foam or balsa core with glass-fibre skins. The lightweight core material also adds useful insulation and built-in buoyancy.

Style of Fit-Out

Interior styling varies from traditional teak to very modern, wipe-clean surfaces of plastic or vinyl, the latter being quite appropriate for the open spaces of a catamaran. To get the best from the catamaran's potential performance, it is best to keep the fit-out as light in weight as possible. This can be done by using a sandwich construction for the interior mouldings or using very thin, veneered ply. One or two companies use items such as vinyl zipped doors instead of timber to cut down on weight.

Choice of Layout or Fit-Out

The use of moulds does restrict the options available to the builder. Some builders will offer options and undertake a certain amount of custom changes to suit

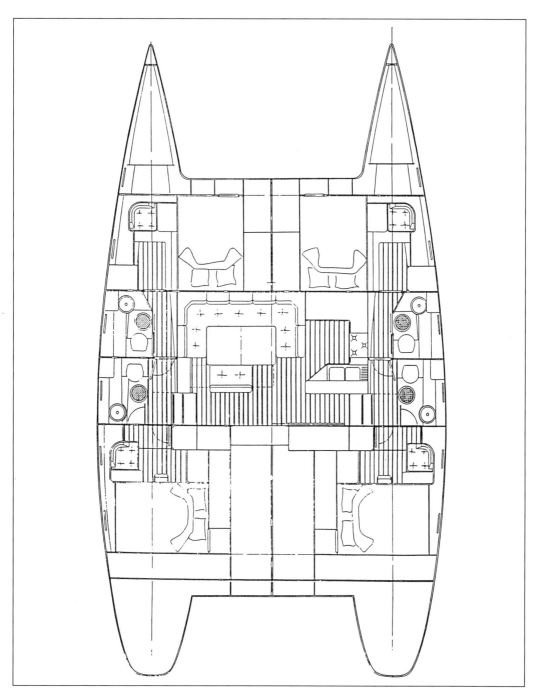

Kennex 42.

individual owners; other builders are set up to produce models which are all identical to each other and the owner's choice may therefore be restricted to no more than the choice of instruments.

Major Catamaran Producers

In what has become a world market, there are far too many producers for them all to be mentioned here. However, the major companies are listed below.

United Kingdom

CATALAC

The Catalac is no longer in production, but I have included it here because there are so many still being sailed and because of the second-hand market. Most Catalacs are bought for their large accommodation areas – they represent a lot of space for the money, and a comfortable ride. The distinguishing feature is the hard chine hull shape without keels. The result is a shallow draft, but not one of the best when the destination is to windward. The Catalac answer in this situation is to turn on the twin diesels – an entirely satisfactory solution for many owners. There are four models at 8m (26ft), 9m (30ft), 10m (33ft) and 12m (39ft).

CLYDE CATAMARANS

The smaller, high-performance Shuttleworth catamarans are produced by Clyde Catamarans.

FANTASY YACHTS

The Woods-designed Strider 26, Banshee 35 and Flice 37 are offered.

The Star-Twins 34.

FREEBIRD

One 15.2m (50ft) model is offered. Even though only a few such cats have been built, Freebird deserves a mention as it is an example of the cat style with good performance and a lot of space.

THE MULTIHULL CENTRE

Building the Summer Twins 25, 28 and 31, aft cabins and central cockpit are a special feature.

MULTIHULL WORLD

This very active company is primarily a sales organization representing a number of British and French builders. The British cats they represent include Patterson and

The Heavenly Twins.

An Event 34.

A Sunbeam 24.

Woods designs. They also operate a catamaran sailing school and charter bookings plus brokerage.

PROUT CATAMARANS
Their range consists of six models from 7.9m (26ft) to 15.2m (50ft). Most follow a similar style, and they have a reputation for being very reliable and safe cruisers. The following features are also found on most of their designs: mast aft rig, nacelle with sonic drive and fixed keels. Most models are of solid glass construction and generally more heavily built than most, although the newer designs use foam sandwich above the water-line.

SEARLE AND WILLIAMS
This small British company has established a niche for itself with a 10m (33ft) power cat that can be used for fishing and other commercial purposes. I have included here as it demonstrates the versatility of the catamaran configuration.

SOLARIS YACHTS
Solaris are a small but well-established company with a well-deserved reputation for high-quality construction and fit-out. With models at 7.3m (24ft), 9.1m (30ft), 9.8m (32ft), 11m (36ft) and 12.2m (40ft), a wide choice is offered.

WHARRAM BUILT
The distinctive James Wharram designs are primarily known for being amateur built. However, a number of different sizes are now available that are built professionally.

All these builders offer their models at various stages of completion.

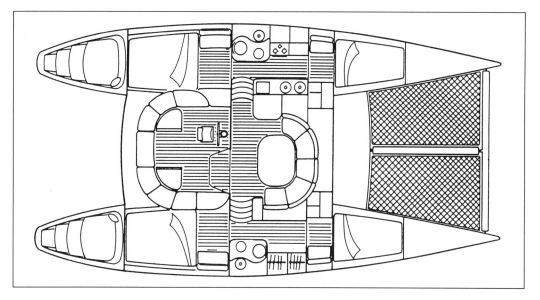

Lagoon 42.

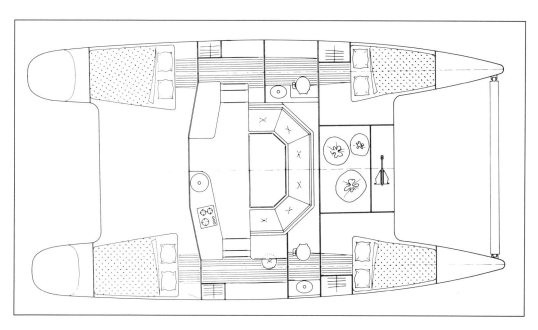

Antigua 37.

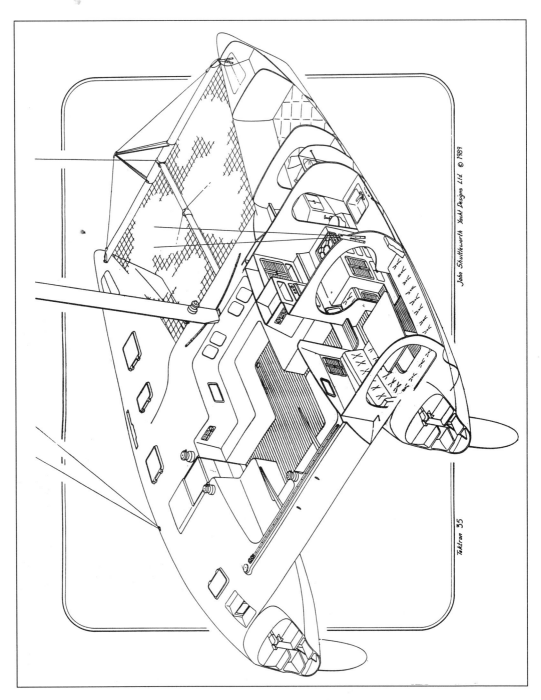

Tektron 35.

France

FOUNTAINE PAJOT

This company has a well-organized factory in Brittany, producing catamarans in considerable numbers. They turn out one 9.8m (32ft) Maldive-class cat every five days. The cats have a typical modern French design, with very rounded decks and coachroof top and an interior style that is quite different to most yachts. There are no options offered. They are simply fitted out and sail well, but the appeal will depend on whether or not you like the distinctive style. However, the numbers sold do testify to their wide appeal to many sailors.

KENNEX

These are high-quality cruisers at 11.5m (38ft) and 12.8m (42ft).

PRIVILEGE

By contrast to Foutaine Pajot, Jeantot Marine have chosen a more traditional timber interior design. The exterior is different in that it looks like a trimaran from above with twin helms aft.

Other Countries

The F-27 is produced in California and is a trailerable trimaran, with folding beam system and good performance. At this size the tri has the advantage of a style of

The Privilege 42.

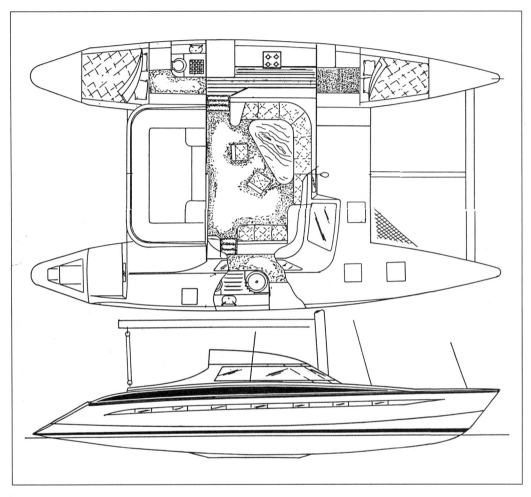

Kelsall 45.

accommodation with good headroom that cannot be fitted within a cat that does not have a bridge-deck saloon. Obviously, the folding beams and trailerability form a unique combination of features that is not available with any other type.

SOUTH AFRICA

South Africa is a country that has taken to the catamaran in a big way. Many companies offer competitive prices.

Designers

Yacht designers tend to specialize in a particular field. It is noticeable that many established designers with reputations in other fields are showing a keen interest in the catamaran configuration. Amongst the newcomers to the profession, most would like to work on the catamaran. The established British designers each have their own particular style and speciality.

A Sagitta 30.

A Tektron 50.

A Mannanan.

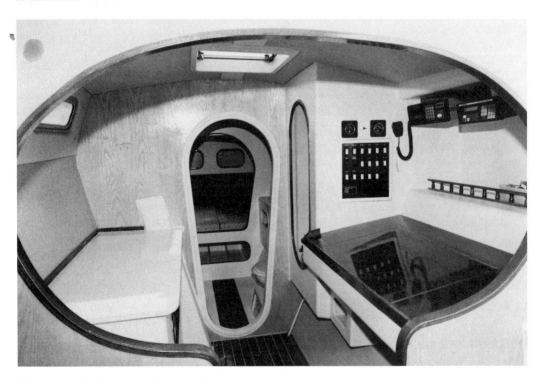

The interior of a Spectrum – in one hull.

Pahi 63 Gaia.

A Banshee.

Custom Designs

As the numbers and choice of standard production designs on the market increase, there are less custom designs built. One reason for choosing a custom design may be for improved sailing or power performance. Another reason may be for the size, particularly if you require a craft over 15m (50ft) long where there is less choice of standard designs, but a vast choice of practical layouts and so on. The larger charter catamarans are often custom-designed and built.

Prout Snowgoose 37 Elite.

SUMMARY

- Catamarans are constructed of glass fibre with a sandwich of PVC foam or balsa core with glass-fibre skins, giving strength and stiffness for minimum weight in many instances.

- All the production builders work in GRP from production moulds. Interior moulds are also used in many cases.

- To get the best from the catamaran's potential performance, it is best to keep the fit-out as lightweight as possible.

10
HOME-BUILT CATAMARANS

Throughout the post-war development of the catamaran and the trimaran, the owner-builder has played an important part and continues to do so. This is partly due to the successful efforts of some designers (who often started as home builders themselves) in promoting their products – James Wharram has been particularly successful in selling his designs in large numbers. It is also partly due to the fact that the professional-built cat was just not available or was restricted to a few models. It is also rather more easy for a builder to imagine the job of building a catamaran with two hulls and a connecting structure rather than tackling the problems of fitting the deep keel of a mono-hull, and coping with the height of the partially completed mono-hull above the ground. I also believe that another factor which is more difficult to define lies in the appeal of the basic catamaran concept to the type of person who is prepared to undertake such a challenging task as building his own yacht.

For those who are prepared to tackle such a project, there is a wide choice of designs and materials available. There is potentially a great deal of money to be saved compared to the market price of the professionally built equivalent, but do not underestimate the commitment required.

Why Build Your Own Catamaran?

Some people build their own boats for the sheer satisfaction of creating a finished article with their own hands. The builder will stand back to view his work at every stage of building with great pride. On the launch date, the long days and evenings of hard work will be totally forgotten. For most owner-builders the reality will be a combination of the need to save money and the creative satisfaction gained.

Cost

The cost of a yacht is very roughly a third each for materials and equipment, for direct labour, and for the builder's overheads and profit. A home builder, not costing his own time and with low overhead costs, can save two-thirds of the price he would pay to sail the same yacht away from a professional yard. By reducing the specification, even further savings can be made – for example, he may be able to find and use some second-hand equipment. It is very unlikely, however, that all this saving could be recovered on a sale, but often building your own cat is the only way you can afford the yacht you want to sail.

The Tiki 28 and Tiki 21.

The Task

Building your own yacht is not an undertaking that should be entered into lightly; it requires almost total dedication. When I did it, I was able to spend all my free time on building a 9.8m (32ft) trimaran. By putting in some very long evenings and weekends I was able to complete it within a year, however, most such one-man projects take much longer. The best approach, if possible, and one which has been adopted most successfully by a number of my customers, is to employ a number of helpers. The number of helpers depends on the size of the craft, with the aim being to complete it within one or two years at the most. Others who also come into this general category are typically businessmen who will employ experienced boat builders and organize the construction themselves, as opposed to working with their own hands. In the case of larger boats and where the owner has the appropriate facilities, this can be a most rewarding exercise.

Building Material

Plywood, with epoxy resin as the adhesive and surfacing material to ensure durability, is the usual choice for most home builders. The advantage is a ready-made, good quality, economical, sheet material

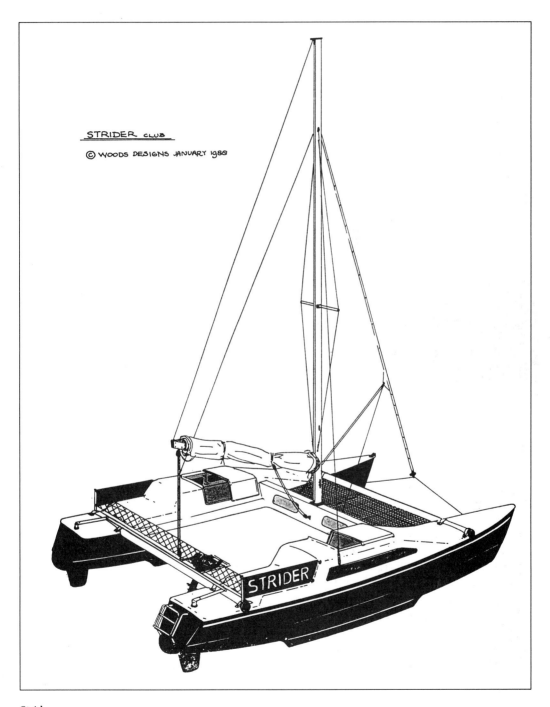

STRIDER CLUB

© WOODS DESIGNS JANUARY 1988

Strider.

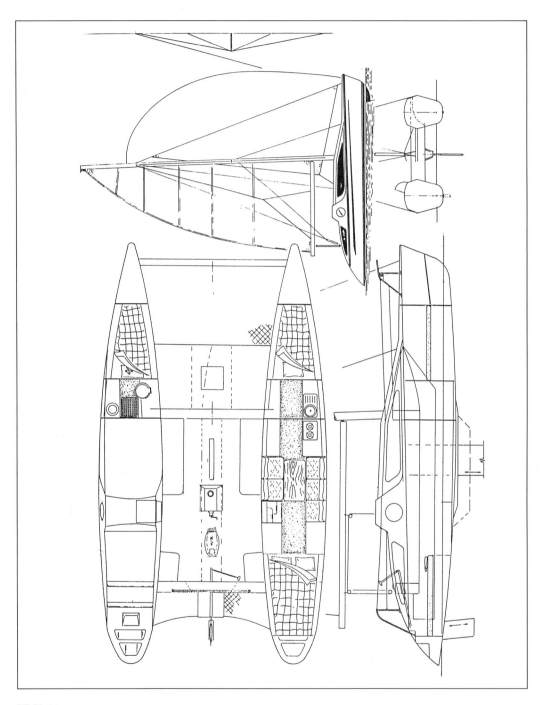

LIMA 34.

The Hitia 17. The igloo tent makes it a camping coastal cruiser.

that is relatively easy and pleasant to work with. The epoxy resin is rather less pleasant and rather expensive to use, but it adds so much to the durability of the finished structure that it is the only sensible way to treat timber.

GRP and GRP/PVC foam materials are available and are very practical alternatives, offering many advantages and usually giving better second-hand value to the finished craft. Contrary to popular opinion, GRP is a most suitable and even forgiving material for the one-off builder. Unless you have previous experience or skills with timber, I suggest that you look very closely at the advantages of GRP and particularly GRP/PVC foam methods. The difference in total cost between the two methods is negligible to the extent that the choice should not be made on cost alone.

Steel is too heavy for the average catamaran, and although aluminium is practical it should only be used by experts.

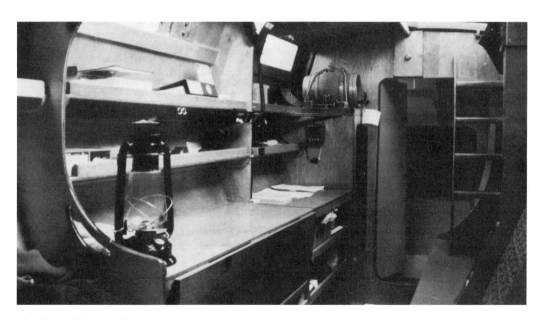

The chart table in a Pahi 42.

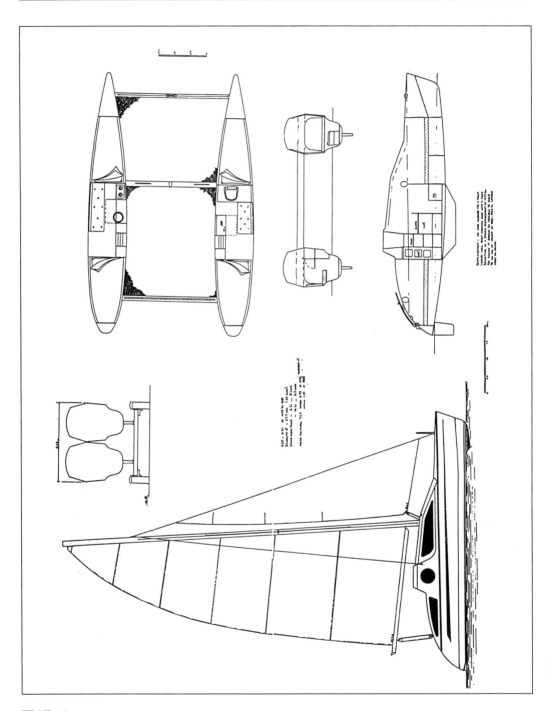

TRAIL 26.

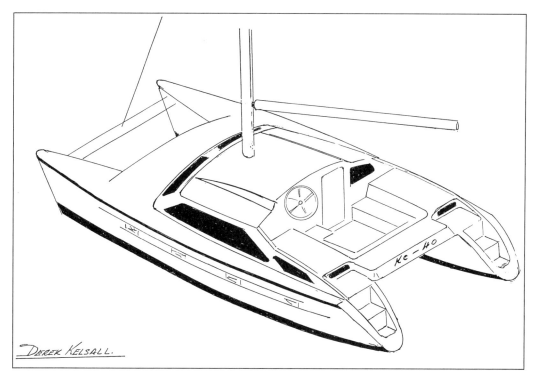

KC-40.

The Plans

A somewhat similar situation exists regarding the cost of plans. There is a wide variation in cost, but as plans costs will not form a major portion of the overall final bill, the choice should be made on whether the design suits best and whether you believe the designer has done all he can to make your job of building as easy as possible. Many designs on offer were drawn ten or twenty years ago, and although such a design may be quite suitable, a more current design may be easier to build due to recent development. An older design may also look dated and hence have a lower second-hand value.

Mistakes

Probably the most common mistakes I see with owner-built catamarans are the 'changes and improvements' made by the owner, often without consulting the designer. A common 'improvement' is to increase the scantlings, but the usual result of this is an overweight catamaran that is less seaworthy.

Internal changes to the layout are usually acceptable. Changes that involve raising coachroofs and the like may give that extra headroom, but they are usually a styling disaster. My approach to this question is to consult the designer first.

117

A Tango 52.

Completing From Mouldings

A popular alternative to starting from scratch, and one which offers some cost savings and less effort, is to complete your craft from a kit of mouldings. Most builders offer this stage as it makes good use of ratio moulds and facilities. The owner will often be able to carry out the interior fitting and equipping to suit his own requirements, and complete the job in a reasonable time. Some builders offer a kit of equipment as well. If you do not opt for this, remember that as there are so many different suppliers involved for all the equipment, you will need to allow some time for paperwork, telephone calls and the like.

SUMMARY

- Building your own catamaran can save up to two-thirds of the cost of buying one from a professional yard.

- Plywood, using epoxy resin as the adhesive and surfacing material to ensure durability, is the usual choice for home builders. GRP and GRP/PVC foam methods are practical alternatives.

- Older designs may be suitable, but more recent ones may be easier to build and will perhaps have a greater second-hand value.

- Before making changes to the design, consult the designer.

11

BUYING A
CATAMARAN

Buying From New

When a yacht is advertised it is always first described by its length – this is the first comparison made whether considering cost or almost any other factor.

For a catamaran, length alone can be very misleading. We have already seen that the usual cat layout and extra beam gives a lot more space than a mono-hull of the same length. When comparing catamarans, beam does vary very considerably and is just as important as length whether comparing accommodation, performance or cost.

It is a relatively simple matter to take the layout drawings and actually measure the plan area of the accommodation. Obviously, length multiplied by beam is a better measurement of the area than simply taking length alone. To illustrate this, I use an example of two 11m (36ft) craft. My first type has been designed with the aim of allowing it to pass through the French canals, and therefore has a beam of less than 5m (16ft). My second type is a typical modern 11m (36ft) craft with no restrictions on beam, and has a 6m (20ft) beam – this comprises a 25 per cent increase in plan area. With similar style accommodation, the catamaran with the 6m (20ft) beam may have as much as 20 per cent more accommodation space. If the two designs are otherwise similar, the extra 122cm (4ft) of width will be very evident in the saloon. The narrow-beam cat also has less stability and, therefore, is likely to have a more moderate rig on a smaller section mast, lighter rigging and so on. With the lower spar cost, less rigging, lighter fittings and less sail area, the difference in cost to the boat builder will be in the order of 20 per cent.

On the important question of cost, the building cost of any yacht is to a large extent a function of the shell surface area. Catamarans have more surface area than a similar single-hull craft, and as a general rule you should expect the same length catamaran to cost more than the same length mono-hull on this count alone. It is certainly less costly to bolt on a ballast keel than to build two hulls. Many cat builders do attempt to compete with mono-hull builders on price, and when the extra accommodation is taken into consideration most cats do represent very good value. A buyer should, however, treat any particularly low price offers with caution.

Each year new catamaran models are launched on to the market, both from established builders and from new companies, thereby offering increased choice to the buyer. One of the first questions is

The Summer Twins.

whether to go for the tried and tested model with, for instance, an established second-hand value, or to go for the latest model that could need further development or could have a better layout than the long-standing design. The buyer must list his requirements in order of preference and match these with the boats on offer.

Trial Sailing

Sales literature can be misleading as virtually all companies claim the same features – lots of space, excellent sailing performance, great stability and so on. Space can be judged by visiting or by comparing scale drawings, but performance under power and sail are more difficult to judge even after you have taken a trial sail because conditions are unlikely to be the same (*see* Chapter 5 for further information on comparing performance).

The 'Try a Multihull' event that is held in Southampton (usually at the end of June each year) is a particularly good venue, providing the opportunity to make direct comparisons on the water. Most catamaran suppliers attend. During the mornings the boats are open for the public to inspect, the builders and sales personnel are on hand if you have any questions. In the afternoon, the visitors are invited to sail aboard as many of the boats as they wish. There is no charge to visitors.

An Antigua 37.

If possible, try to visit a cat in cruising trim, with all the owner's possessions on board. This will help assess the practicality of stowage arrangements and carrying capacity. A common failing of many cruising catamarans is the lack of provision for stowage, particularly deck stowage, and poor allowance for the extra weight of cruising gear. Check the water-line when the boat is fully loaded – if it has disappeared below the water-level it is not likely to be the best choice for long-distance cruising.

The three very simple formulae given in Chapter 5 can be used to make comparisons of speed under sail, speed under power and stability. You will need to know the sail area, the height of the centre of effort of the sailplan, the weight, the distance from the centreline to the centreline of the lee hull and the weight. The builder or designer should be able to provide these figures. Weight is the figure that is most difficult to confirm, and the best way to check it is to compare the actual water-line with that given in the drawings. Treat any claims for extremely low weight and a resultant improved performance with a degree of scepticism.

The cat is often sold on performance. However, most producers tend to concentrate on the accommodation aspect so that performance inevitably suffers to some extent. The potential owner, for whom the sailing performance is very important, should be particularly careful when making his choice of both the model of catamaran and its specification. If at all possible and you are in any doubt, the time and money spent on chartering a catamaran will be well spent. There are several options to charter in many parts of Europe.

Custom-Built Boats

Many builders offer the custom-built option, particularly for craft over 13.7m (45ft) where the numbers of standard designs on offer are limited and where the catamaran configuration offers such a variety of choice. The owner who wishes to choose his own layout, sailing performance, power performance, style of fit-out, construction material and so on will find a number of quality catamaran builders who will all be very willing to undertake such projects.

With today's ease of travel and communication it is feasible to have your yacht built almost anywhere in the world – from almost any country in Europe to places as far away as New Zealand and Argentina. A country that has taken to the catamaran in a very big way is South Africa where a wide choice of builders offer every type and size at very competitive prices. Again, the caution is to check out each builder thoroughly before making a commitment.

Second-Hand Catamarans

There is an ever-increasing market in second-hand cats, but it is still restricted in choice compared to that for mono-hull due to the small number of manufacturers and production models available in the past. The first advice is to make up a short list of possible craft and examine each one thoroughly. If possible, have a trial sail, preferably in a breeze, and ensure that everything is in working order. If you can find an experienced cat sailor to accompany you, all the better. 'Do not buy without a survey' is just as important a maxim with a cat as with any other craft. If the cat is on a mooring or in a marina, it is also important to check if there are any outstanding debts against the boat – if you buy the boat you will be responsible.

What to Look For

BUILDING MATERIALS

GRP is the usual and most durable material used in catamaran construction. However, osmosis is a term affecting GRP which is heard and read about extensively. GRP catamarans are just as likely to suffer from this complaint as any other GRP boat. Look for blisters under the anti-fouling usually just at the water-line. When broken, the blister will be found to be full of water with an acidic smell. If a few blisters are found they are fairly easily dealt with and should not necessarily preclude a purchase.

The potential buyer should also look for cracks in the gel coat around the edges of coachroof or coamings, for any movement in the bulkheads and at the general condition of any inside stiffeners, particularly below floorboards. If the trouble spot is accessible, GRP is a relatively easy material to repair and strengthen. Although GRP is an extremely durable material and there are many very good 25-year-old catamarans still sailing, the age of the catamaran is important for many reasons – from its expected useful life, to the availability of spares and the styling.

If you are considering buying a timber catamaran then it is even more important to get an expert opinion. If there is a problem it is likely to be in the most inaccessible place and it is important to know where to look.

BRIDGE-DECK CLEARACE

Bridge-deck clearance is mentioned in Chapter 3, but is worth discussing again here. Many of the early catamarans were given rather less bridge-deck clearance than is usual today. The same applies to the overall beam of the cat.

WEIGHT AND CARRYING CAPACITY

Weight and carrying capacity are important factors. A figure that is relevant is the kilograms emersion per cm. Figures taken from typical cruising styles are as follows:

```
 7.3m (24ft) cat – 88kg/cm
 8.2m (27ft) cat – 110kg/cm
10.4m (34ft) cat – 144kg/cm
12.2m (40ft) cat – 188kg/cm
13.7m (45ft) cat – 230kg/cm
15.8m (52ft) cat – 320kg/cm.
```

From these figures you can see that a 10.4m (34ft) craft that is floating 10cm (4in) below its lines will be nearly 1.5 tonne over its designed displacement. Narrow-beam hulls will be rather more susceptible to overloading, and it is easy to see how simple it is to overload the smaller catamaran. Overloading will immediately affect performance and bridge-deck clearance, but whether there is any danger will depend on a number of factors such as the degree of overloading and structural strength. In the extreme, questions such as reserve buoyancy will come into play. A small amount of overloading, however, should not adversely affect a strongly built cat.

DISPLACEMENT

There is often some confusion over the use of the term displacement. Displacement is the weight of water that is displaced by the floating catamaran. The designed displacement is the weight of water that is displaced by the catamaran floating at the drawn water-line. The figure that we are interested in is the actual weight of the boat plus the payload and where the water-line will be at that weight – this figure may be quite different from the designer's estimate. There are many instances of designers being over-optimistic about the weight of the finished catamaran, the result being that the water-lines have had to be repainted. At the other end of the scale, a designer may decide to make generous allowance for load carrying, and the figure given as designed displacement may therefore be rather more than the true sailing weight. This latter approach is the preferable of the two. A catamaran with a relatively high designed displacement is not necessarily a heavy catamaran, but is a better vehicle for sailing when lighter than the designed displacement rather than the other way round. To make any kind of realistic comparison you need the true built weight of the craft.

AMATEUR-BUILT CATAMARANS

With the large number of amateur-built cats about, you have to be particularly careful when making your choice. The fact that a cat has been built by an amateur need not deter you as some are excellent. Some of these types will be made of ply while others will be made of GRP/PVC foam. Older ply boats, often built with a skin of glass and polyester resin, will be near the end of their useful lives. Where the ply and timber has been protected with the correct epoxy treatment, the life of the boat is extended considerably.

GRP/PVC foam cats should be every bit as durable as any other GRP cat with the added advantage of built-in insulation. The standard of finish of some of the owner-built foam sandwich cats leaves a lot to be desired, but this should not rule out all foam sandwich craft. Done correctly, the foam sandwich is the best method of construction and is currently the first choice for most professional as well as home builders. However, not all marine surveyors are familiar with sandwich construction methods and materials. You will need someone who is if you are to get a true assessment.

YOUR FIRST BOAT

If the catamaran is your first cruising boat, as is often the case, you need to decide which type of craft is most suitable for your needs. Perhaps the first question you should ask yourself is whether the accent will be on performance or accommodation. The styling, the type of auxiliary power, the type of rig, the cost and so on will all also come into the equation. The second-hand value of a craft is of importance to a majority of potential owners, and this tends to direct the choice in favour of long-established designs such as a Prout that has an established value for its year and condition. This approach could eliminate the more modern, wider beam, higher bridge-deck clearance-style cats that have come into the fore only in more recent years – fewer are for sale and the market value is more difficult to predict.

A number of people have fallen into the trap of buying an ex-racing boat or a part-finished boat at a 'bargain' price. The latter in particular can be tempting as, what is on offer often looks like a lot of boat for the money. The points to remember here, however, are that the hull will usually represent no more than 20 per cent of the total cost, completion will almost certainly take more time and money than anticipated, and if necessary work is done on a less-than-perfect hull, the finished craft will never be better than the base from which you started.

Newcomers to catamaran sailing often say that they are not at all interested in performance and this may be true. However, many such owners have been known to change their views on this after just a few outings. I can remember my introduction to sailing very well – it was in an interesting harbour in North Africa. Sailing conditions were superb most of the time and there were always new things to see and explore. I was not at all interested in getting involved in chasing other boats around the harbour – that was until I was persuaded to make up numbers on one occasion, and from then on I was hooked. Racing opened up a whole new interest in sailing for me. The same can apply to anyone who enters a cruising cat in local club races, so the warning is that you should take note of sailing performance if there is any chance that you may develop this interest.

SUMMARY

- Decide your list of requirements in order of preference and try to match this as closely as possible with the boats on offer.

- If possible, visit the catamaran in cruising trim and with all the owner's possessions on board. Check the water-line when fully loaded. If it has disappeared below the water-level it is not likely to be the best choice for long-distance cruising.

12
CONCLUSION

When the first catamarans took part in the Single-Handed Transatlantic Race in 1964, the designers and sailors were unsure of the cat's capabilities to the extent that they fitted ballast keels and masthead buoyancy in order to achieve self-righting from a knock down. In contrast to this, the catamarans crossing the Atlantic in the 1990s do so in complete confidence, and the ballast keels and masthead buoyancy have been replaced by a wider beam, sea-anchors and drogues.

Catamarans are not for everyone. However, every open-minded individual who is involved with or is considering getting involved with cruising should at least give the catamaran serious thought. If you are looking for regular weekend racing as well as cruising, however, a mono-hull will almost certainly suit you best.

Look for a catamaran that really does make the best use of its twin-hull configuration. This includes features from designs that make it easy to walk around the yacht from transom steps, to wide side-decks, a view from the saloon seating, good ventilation, a home-sized galley, and berths that can be left unmade during the day, not to mention the sailing advantages.

If you are a newcomer to catamarans and do not have the chance to charter or sail with a school, I suggest that you attempt to contact a catamaran owner near you. You will almost certainly find him to be very proud of his yacht and to be more than willing to show you around it and to talk over his experiences. MOCRA can always help in this respect.

If you are an experienced mono-hull sailor who decides that the catamaran is worth a try, you will almost certainly never go back. If you decide the catamaran is for you, you will be joining an ever-growing band of catamaran enthusiasts who will ensure that the catamaran configuration will continue to expand in numbers and acceptance.

GLOSSARY

Bear away   To turn away from the wind.
Bilge   The space in the hull under the cabin sole.
Bimini   A folding cockpit cover.
Bridge-Deck   The decking between the two hulls of a catamaran.

Catamaran   A twin-hulled craft. The hulls are usually identical.
Clew of Sail   The aft lower corner of a triangular sail.
Coachroof   The structure over the saloon of a catamaran.
Cockpit   The area, usually aft of the main saloon, from which most sail controls are handled. The outside seating area.
Cruising chute   A spinnaker-style headsail that is sheeted like a Genoa.
Cruising racing   A style of catamaran designed for best sailing performance but with sufficient accommodation for comfortable cruising.
Cutter   Single mast with two headsails – the yankee and staysail.

Drogue   A drag device that is trailed to slow the vessel's speed.

Escape hatch   Usually a deck hatch that is set into the side of the catamaran hull.

Genoa   The large headsail, usually hanked on to the forestay or in a headsail roller system.
Gel coat   The pigmented outside coat of a GRP boat.
GRP   Glass-reinforced polyester. There are two basic types: orthothalic is used for most GRP structures; isothalic is more water-resistant and is used for gel coats and for some hulls.

Hard chine   A hull shape made from panels.
Head of sail   The top corner of a triangular sail.
Hounds   The mast fitting to which the forestay fitting is attached.

Ketch   Main mast forward, smaller mast aft.

Luff   To luff is to turn the yacht towards the wind. The sails will flap as they point into the wind.

Mainsail   The sail that is aft of the mast and usually attached to the mast with slides in a track.
Mizzen staysail   A sail flown from the head of the mizzen mast to approximately the foot of the mainmast of a ketch rig.
Motor-sailer   Yacht which is equipped with rig and sails but which also has a large engine or engines to achieve good performance under engine alone.

Nacelle   A section of the bridge-deck that is lower than the main bridge-deck area. It is usually hull-shaped.

Osmosis   Water penetration through the gel coat and into the laminate below. Blistering can occur on hulls after they have been in the water for some time.

Parachute anchor   A parachute that is used in the water to stop drift.

Preventer   A line or tackle tieing the boom down to the rail.

Proa   A two-hulled craft with a main hull and outrigger.

PVC foam   Polyvinyl chloride foam. A tough, resilient foam that is not affected by water.

Reach   To sail with the true wind at approximately 90 degrees to the direction of sailing.

Round up   To turn into the wind.

Run   To sail with the wind from astern.

Sheets   The lines used to control the sails.

Sloop   A single headsail on forestay to the masthead.

Sonic drive   A drive unit that allows the prop to be steered and lifted. SONIC is the name used by the manufacturer.

Spinnaker   A lightweight balloon-style sail that is flown from the mast when the wind is from astern.

Staysail   The aft sail of a double headsail rig.

Surf   To sail on the front of a wave.

Tack of sail   The forward lower corner of a triangular sail.

Tide-rode   To lie at anchor with bow facing into the tide.

Trampoline   Fabric material used in the space between the hulls.

Trimaran   Three hulls, with two smaller outer hulls.

Vang   A fitting that controls the angle of the boom to the mast.

Warps   Lines used to tie the yacht to the quayside or marina.

Wind-rode   To lie at anchor with bow to wind. (Tide may be in opposing direction.)

Yankee   The forward sail of a double headsail rig.

INDEX